Mediterranean Perspective

CLAUDIO NARDI

DESIGN MEDIA PUBLISHING (UK) LIMITED

CONTENTS

Claudio Nardi

The Architect is a figure which embraces social and cultural roles, researching and creating new trends. Claudio Nardi graduated from the School of Arts of Carrara, and therefore came from an art school formation, which at the time was the basis for the active preparation of creative thought and new design, in an Italy that was the centre of innovation and research, where creativity and cultivated crafts were the fulcrum of Italian presence in the world.

Nardi's education and formal training was not limited to the study. He apprenticed at Poltronova, a workshop of ideas and experimentation, a space where the most important Italian design architects of the moment such as Superstudio, Archizoom, Sottsass, De Pas D'Urbino Lomazzi found a platform of expression and who subsequently played an irreplaceable role in innovation in design and the quality of life in the world. In Poltronova, Nardi began to have contacts with his first clients interpreting their thoughts and desires, offering interior furnishings, inserting objects from the workshop made of new materials and shapes. Happy and fresh ideas stimulated his young creativity and made customers happy.

It was at this stage that his fundamental relationship with artisans was born and structured. A relationship that has never been interrupted, representing a continuous moment of growth and training. It was this close relationship with the craftsmen that helped shape his ideas and his research. Nardi believes that the true tutors, in all his training as an architect, were them, the artisans.

He came into contact with Carlo Scarpa when he started collaborating with International Design, an innovative furniture store in Florence, which became an icon in the world of contemporary furnishings. The relationship with Carlo Scarpa was born with the project of the International Design building in via delle Mantellate in Florence, where Scarpa promoted the use of Nardi's project for the lighting design instead of his own.

During this period he was also studying for his degree at the University of Architecture of Florence, which he thought was not in step with the times and of no particular stimulus. He graduated with an innovative project that recalled the Cuban Revolution, travelling education, a "library bus" to bring knowledge to the world touching the intimate places and souls in every territory even the most remote, bringing a ray of knowledge to everyone in order to not be oppressed, but to become "prepared" to live on the same social level. It was with this spirit that this fresh graduate began measuring himself with small projects entering the intimacies of homes, spaces, and people.

Through International Design, he met Andrea Panconesi, for whom he designed the Luisa Via Roma store in Florence. Thanks to this meeting and the revolutionary nature of the project, it gave him a very important opportunity to enter the world of high fashion and design. Nardi, because of his talent and vision, became one of the first protagonists in the fusion of fashion and design in the 1980s, developing research for this sector that mirrored the foundations of the new way to live retail interiors exemplified by the design of Luisa in Via Roma in Florence. The project was born both from the reinterpretation of

Opening of the Exhibition "Claudio Nardi Architects Multiplicity of Beauty" – Pisa (Italy), 17 October 2014

external space and interior space closing off the shop from the street and the analysis of the problems and needs of the products proposed and sold in the various spaces. The fashion collaborations didn't end there. He then began the design of the unique experimental fashion concept store SBAIZ, in Lignano Sabbiadoro. This commission consolidated his experience with master artisans and the world of the great artisan culture that was present in Tuscany at that time. It was through the fashion world that he was introduced to Dolce and Gabbana, who were just beginning their ascent, and with them he began to design their retail spaces around the world, uniting his creativity and vision to their high fashion creativity into a singular and overwhelming success, shared by a captivated public. Other fashion designers also became clients such as Ferré, Valentino, Tod's and many independent concept stores in Italy and around the world, with recent projects in Singapore, Hanoi, and Saigon.

From 1986/87, the Nardi studio started entering architectural competitions, and thus began the search for an appropriate language which could always meet different criteria and locations. It is with this rigour and cleanliness that he has approached many different themes, such as the competition for the New University Residency in Rome in 2003 (special mention) where he imagined an almost underground architecture, embedded into the banks of the Tiber, where ancient construction materials, such as natural terracotta and sunlight, outlined constantly mutating forms and atmospheres. Among the first prizes: the 1996 Urban Reconstruction Competition at Campi Bisenzio; 1998 Redefinition Piazza Matteotti in Tavarnelle Val di Pesa; 2002 Port Authority of Marina di Carrara; 2001 Hotel Monginevro in Florence; 2002 Lungomare of Lignano Sabbiadoro; the new building complex for the Kraków City Council in Poland and the Museum of Contemporary Art in Krakow, made possible by the recovery of the former Schindler factory, where the exterior and interior dialogue in a continuous succession of glimpses of open skies creating spatial relationships that conduct the visitor on a stroll through contemporary art.

From furnishings to competitions, to the design of houses to more complex buildings, there is always a consistent philosophy. Nardi considers that starting from the interior design process was fundamental in order to know and understand the very function of architecture. From inner space, from the soul, one moves to the design of the casing, to the skin that will cover it, leaving the artifact to have the possibility of future transformations. The figure of the Architect in the evolution of society is linked to the possibility of granting a quality of living to the flexibility of transformation depending on the mutation of the needs while maintaining the quality of the functions. Also very important is the the approach, a total vision of the project as a "cinematic" imagination, to see the project come to life, inserted into its context, lived with opportunities for change over time, through modest changes in spaces and functions. Therefore, each project is born "exclusive" for that space, for that area, to meet those needs, "I believe," Nardi says, "changing the suburbs in their redevelopment through small interventions: creating openings, closing openings, adding or subtracting small volumes, colours and materials, incorporating energy-enhancing technologies, inserting green areas, public spaces, always using small steps, entering the core of the initial project and then adjusting it according to new needs. All this in favour of improving the quality of life through small transformations, a 'homeopathy of architecture'."

This possibility of continuous transformation of spaces and places should reflect the changing needs of the users in what Nardi calls "Re-Architecture". So we ask ourselves what happens if in anonymous buildings we make transformations for individual parts, even in modest ways? Does the visual perception and consequently its value also change?

Nardi has a great respect for the Renaissance and for the philosophy that "to understand the body it is necessary to analyse the organs" in an operation. It is essential for the work of the designer to start from the soul, from the internal organs, to approach and grow outside. Simultaneously he also maintains that rationalism has provided great lessons and has been of fundamental importance in the mutation of our contemporary society.

Social intimacy.

Claudio Nardi does not conceive projects on the drawing board. Before any expression, he "imagines the signs" and "sees" the finished idea, tracing the lines to form a mental perspective. Only then Nardi begins to develop his designs creating hand-drawn perspectives, which explore in detail all the elements of the finished space, and then with his collaborators verifies and defines the project. In effect, Nardi argues that every project requires an in-depth analysis and the correction of errors is fundamental in order to "grow", to arrive at the end: "to create a product that I am satisfied with".

To do this, Nardi, a multi-faceted architect, calls upon all parts of himself, born of his various experiences and culture, to address the design theme without forgetting to express all those different characters and disciplines which intersect in forming an architectural uniqueness. Each project requires its own in-depth analysis, a story that is very explicit through the organisation of that image, something which is never superficial.

Certainly the humility that is found in Claudio is fundamental to a project with satisfaction and success; "one needs to understand and deprive oneself of presumptions to achieve results."

Nardi's architectural process of working on different plans demonstrates an architectural design quest approaching the essential soul of the project by degrees, through stages, arriving at a complete resolution of the functions and the justification of the choices made for its realisation. Claudio Nardi is an architect of our time who understands the purity of form and the inclusion of clean volumes.

arch. Maurizio Andruetto, arch. Monica Deri

> *"In the place of the deepest obscurity, between the menacing shadows, beauty and love will save us by indicating the path."*

Between Design and City

Interview with Claudio Nardi
by arch. massimo del seppia-associazione LP
m.d. September 2014

Formation and influences

1. How did you live your childhood and formative years? Family, school and university, Prato and then Florence.

Billy Elliot springs to mind. I moved timidly and quite silently in a dynamic world made of raw materials, laborious and repetitive work, very noisy, a constant racket of rapid and determined movements... The noise of the city was always very loud: the endless drumming of weaving looms, voices shouting over the din... It all reverberated around me in my ideal little world (the attic) where I played, creating imaginary worlds made of found things, little bits of wood, old boxes of detergent defended by the same toy soldiers that used to come in the detergent (the mythical Tide). In short, I was always making models. When I think about my father, a weaver in Prato, for as long as I can remember, he was always at the loom fourteen hours a day. Not withstanding that, I think of the subtle, timid natural elegance of the 50's and 60's, my period of reference. Nevertheless, at that time, I found Prato very restrictive and as soon as I could, throwing away with no regret two years of science studies, I began life as a commuter attending the Art Institute at Porta Romana in Florence. This was my only true school, and with the aid of Professor Conti in the role of Professor Keating (Dead Poets Society) I began to see what I was really looking for... Immediately following that at seventeen years old I began my experience at Poltronova as an "interior design consultant" chosen by Sergio Camilli who was the owner and creator of Poltronova (the revolutionary furniture and producer of the 60's and 70's). The first clients, little projects, unripe ideas, in a place frequently visited by such designers as Ettore Sottsass, Gae Aulenti, Superstudio, Archizoom, Carlo Scarpa, Gavina... (a kind of Mediterranean Bauhaus)

Then, I did my final studies and final Art exams in Carrara as a private student to avoid wasting more time. There I was adopted by Puccio Duni, my lifelong tutor. He gave me a job initially at his Design Centre and then at International Design of Florence, where I worked, designing and learning (simultaneously I was studying architecture at University, which left only modest traces in my formation). It was here that I had the opportunity to meet Carlo Scarpa and to "collaborate" as his assistant on the design and construction of the International Design showroom and building. I would go and visit him at Valmarana; we would talk; he would design; I would dine with him and his wife, sleeping in the limonaia (a building where the lemon trees were stored during the winter). I had become a small project manager but for Carlo Scarpa, he always made it all seem something very normal and relaxed...

2. Why did you decide to study architecture and then become an architect ?

In the easiest and most antique way. When I as a kid (maybe ten years old), they would ask me what I wanted to be when I grew up? An Architect! Did I know what it really meant? Who knows? Slowly and slowly the idea did take form, by itself, corresponding with attitudes, passions, the attractions of transforming and humanising of nature.

3. How was your debut into the profession of Architect, the first projects?

Very much a path of self instruction. I trusted myself to sensory perceptions, instincts about space, place, form, even reason and history... Not having learnt a methodology apprenticing from a maestro, I made my own path... Observations, errors, successes, learning, emotions, synthesis.

4. Looking at your work, I remain fascinated by your success into the world of interior design and in consequence in the fashion world. What were the important first projects and how did you first enter the fashion world?

Everything happened very early. It was the early 80's, the birth of the fashion world as we know it. Italian fashion, English fashion, Japanese fashion... I was in at the beginning, talented, and my friend and mentor Puccio Duni introduced me to Andrea Panconesi, who was launching Luisa Via Roma in the olympus of reference points for world fashion, so I won the small competition, and designed the new store of LUISA VIA ROMA in 1984. From that success followed many commissions all over Italy and around the world. Clients such as Dolce and Gabbana who were just starting in 1988, Valentino, Tod's, Malo, Ferrè... It was a happy dominion with many other projects for interiors and residential architecture, but, as I always say, I don't like specialisation and so I worked to establish myself in other fields like competitions and therefore pursue the grand architecture...

5. Successively in what way do you relate with modern Italian design and what weight has the Italian rationalist architecture of the 1920's had in your formation?

In the same way in which one chooses the music one loves, one chooses, like women, simply one concedes, one becomes permeable to emotions, and I have become aware of that which has been taking root inside long after my first proper engagements with architecture... It is also true that, already then, in an époque which was coveting the "minimalism" of Pawson, Italian rationalism represented the solution, an elevated synthesis that is simultaneously easy to understand, viable, reproducible, reassuring, for both client and architect... Rationalism and the Mediterranean architecture of our roots.

6. Which figure in the Italian panorama of the last century do you consider fundamental?

Well, really I can't define the master of our époque. Maybe a little out of ignorance? Between the various figures I would say Carlo Scarpa and Giò Ponti, because one represented the synthesis between artisan knowledge, humble yet rich in its sublime past... an idea of space that is simultaneously modern and classical and also the perfect synthesis between interior space and architecture, and the second because he was the pioneer of the meeting between new and traditional materials as he explored new formal expressions in the design of interiors, in architecture, in objects for manufacturing; he anticipated and personified modernity.

7. Can you tell me what you consider to be the five masterpieces of architecture of all time?

Tate Modern (Herzog & De Meuron), because it is the perfect example of Re-architecture; Villa Malaparte (Libera), because it transforms thought and nature into architecture; the Barcelona

Pavilion (Mies), because it recounts the poetry of mathematics, of geometry, of purity and elegance; the Chrysler Building (Van Alen), because it blends the concept of decoration with acceleration; the Pantheon, because it is the absolute.

8. Like a laboratory we concern ourselves with every form of cultural expression. Can you tell me some of your references in cinema, music, painting and other fields? Does a work exist that has had a profound influence on your world?

Quintet and Dogville, Mozart and Leonard Cohen, Caravaggio and Rothko. There are many others, obviously, which make up my reference of imagery, but these are the first that spring to mind and, I realise now: I look for an artistic expression which on one side has richness and sophisticated abundance, and on the other ascetic and complex purity. This is the combination which inspires me. Almost forty years ago I was very attracted by Boullée, the one from Greenaway's "The Belly of the Architect", and then the panorama became much more varied, open... The monument ceased to become an absolute necessity.

Philosophy

9. What relationship do you have with architectural history? How do you relate to the works of the great masters of the past? How do you insert your work in historic contexts?

Above all I am fascinated by architecture as a living organism, which transforms places and continues to transform itself autonomously, mutating, and in this the great masters have an important role

Works in progress of the MOCAK Museum – Krakow (Poland), March 2009

but it isn't necessarily fundamental. The passions, the revolutions, discoveries, economies, politics, collective spirit, the great minds, it all makes history and also the architecture, in ways both good and bad... With this perspective having the opportunity to work in a historic centre or context is exhilarating, as you can take part as protagonists at this continual and ceaseless breathing of architecture and men.

10. In our manifesto, we exhort knowledge and ban all forms of superficiality and waste, which unfortunately, seems to be very widespread: what does knowledge mean to you?

The waste, in my opinion, is in everything that does not work and does not thrill. It is in everything that's ugly (it's like a thin venom that creates an addiction) and knowledge should always be at the service of passion and beauty; I would like beauty to find its mathematical unit of measurement ... like the one that regulates the balance of chemistry and living beings; all the alibi would fall and we would see that cold knowledge can produce monsters, like those produced by the 70's style urban philosophy. Certainly a hedonic and superficial approach has produced the Post Modern (horrible, but has done less damage or at least not irreversible).

11. In your projects I always find a line and a personal guiding principle; I would like you to express to me your point of view on the situation of contemporary architecture.

Contemporary architecture in my opinion... a conscious architecture of the past, of the context, but is not indulgent or hides in citations; an architecture that explores the technological evolution of materials and systems and knows how to make the right choices each time between traditional or innovative techniques , or the merging of the two, which is not only intended to induce an easy and facile astonishment, which is not only self-referential, which does not forget the sense of function, which is not ephemeral, which is made to last but also for change and transformation.

12. Personally I am facing a journey to discover the true roots of our contemporary architecture and my answer is increasingly the Italian rationalism of the 1920s; architects like Figini and Pollini, Bottoni, Terragni and Libera, but also Luigi Moretti and BBPR; I would like your opinion on this approach, if you share it and what today should be revaluated and resumed.

Italian rationalism (but also anonymous Mediterranean architecture) as a root and a tracer for the contemporary ... a tracer that remains actual ... still fertile ... open to infinite reinterpretations, transformations, uses, perfect for one to learn about their own means and even their own limits,

an abacus and a language that can be the basis of personal and stylistic growth without becoming the point of landing, even more... In this view I find it incomprehensible that the most beautiful architecture in the world in the 20th century (and I also include the original interpretations adopted in Italian Colonial Territories) has no attention, exhibitions, studies, or universal consecration.

13. Which of your projects expresses best your design philosophy? Put in another way, in what project have you been able to fully express your thoughts?

Certainly Luisa Via Roma in Florence; I have revised it so many times and the original version introduced a big innovation in the Florentine and Italian landscape not only in the approach to design, because it was a work of interior architecture and not just because interior architecture became a façade, the façade became a backdrop and the space had a whole complex and complete history.

The fact that I did it last time in 2008 after 25 years is fun! Provide new materials, new words, new attitudes to the same space;then the experience I had with Dolce and Gabbana; then some competition projects, not least that of Krakow that are very interesting. Then Mocak, Riva Lofts, BP Studio, Port Authority Headquarters...

14. I greatly appreciate your new-dandy concept, that is, the need for beauty as a primary requirement. This concept is strongly present in our manifesto. What is your idea of beauty?

Beauty must become or rather has to become a necessity, and the subjective perception of beauty and its relativity must cease to be an alibi to dismantle criticism, to lower the attention, to pass the worst abonimations, but only to represent the overcoming, in positive, shared common perception, "the canon" that no longer exists today... through the strength and supremacy of excellence, as happened and happens, but not always, in the art world.

The need for beauty must become a primary need and not an aristocratic need. New-dandy, because it is about shared beauty, accessible and all-embracing, a beauty that is not exclusively industrial (directed by the media) which has become the only perceived beauty, instead, is a subtle beauty, which is subtracted from calculation and market, which can only be felt, tried, like happiness, not only in the great works but also and above all in the everyday landscape, from the grand horizons to the small ones.

15. The Architect also, because of the excessive bureaucracy, is increasingly becoming a lost technocrat and in my opinion is losing the nature of his essence; I believe that the humanistic aspect is indispensable and plays a fundamental role as knowledge, experience and talent. How important is this for you in your work and in your life?
How true that is! They are killing us! I think that having to deal with limits, strict and complex conditions can also represent an opportunity for wealth and complexity and opportunities for brilliant solutions, but sometimes, without being able to count on partners, who are specialised in handling the bureaucratic process, you really can see the creative vein cut down to zero ... and this is

an epochal damage!

Cities

16. What do you think of urban planning today and what is your idea of a City for Mankind?
Borders have become indefinite (and not just as a game of words) until they touch each other and happen not only for the city concept, but for nations, for peoples, for ethics, for the costumes of society and it is not said that it is necessarily a bad thing.

From the growth of urban agglomerations and their melting, new artificial centres such as "shopping malls" inevitably arise or older smaller areas return to life.

I have long lost, if I have ever had it, confidence in the possibilities of urban planning to solve the problems of the city or to find and renew it. Perhaps it is not worth to deepen the argument except to emphasise what the "Planning" has underestimated, that is, the value of Beauty, Architecture, Harmony, that is, the basic needs and duties, as well as the material ones that are subject to the struggles of a century, the right to seek happiness, not just standards.

It may mean, in our case, to save the built sites or preserve the ones still intact or to recover the ones that are no longer used and nevertheless to dare...

17. What do you think about involvement in the urban planning process? Can there be true democracy in architecture?
It would lead you to wonder what democracy

means today, but maybe we would be heading off track. I would say that no. It struggles to exist. I also say that sometimes it exists and sometimes it does damage, like how the speculators cause damage, or how superficiality causes damage. The lack of democracy in architecture is not the main drama, the Magnificent Lords no longer exist and there is no shared sentiment of the common good, even less of beauty, of her values, nor even the value of the creative violation of her canons. Everything is confused, everything seems acceptable and beautiful according to some. Instead, we should become more demanding (intolerant?), but also have to learn to accept and govern anarchy, that passionate, creative and extraordinary beauty.

18. The topic of recovery of abandoned areas is today very current, also in Italy and a strongly felt subject. Re-architecture, the theme of building within the already built, can be a cue for their recovery? What is your thinking about the possibilities for their recovery? What does it mean for you to recover, to re-enhance a district or any part of a city that has lost or has never had its vital energy?
Along with the architecture of new and large sustainable works of our urban landscape, a multitude of interventions or micro-interventions could make extraordinary and happy transformations in the urban fabric, in the "peripheries", in the abandoned areas, but also in the historic centres.

It is precisely the theme of Re-architecture, of modifying that which is already built, of handling with care, which has always been part of our culture, at least until the 1960's ... an ancient and consolidated attitude to the confrontation with the stratifications, the use of ancient words that combine with new materials and new balance, through interventions ranging from "maquillage" (renewed materials, colours or finishes) to the invention of a new "dress" through the creation of ventilated facades, new "skins" light and the technological, up to "aesthetic surgery"... with small or large additions or subtractions or transformations of parts into form and function.

I am always fascinated by the concept of transformation. The strength and beauty of transformation and the human body is the most appropriate of the allegories, and above all thinking of architecture, contains and expresses functions, emotions and intentions, constantly changes and naturally accepts transformations. It can be modified and led to interpreting different roles and tales, adapting to the times, the modes and the aesthetics of the age; can be manipulated in a variety of ways, always lightening, softening, hardening, through make-up, surgery, addiction, subtraction, colour, skin, dress... and it is so obvious that the same manipulations can be easily objected to the buildings.

A valid argument for buildings and cities in general, especially for disused buildings, for outskirts and suburbs.

I am firmly convinced that, from a functional, aesthetic, technical, and environmental point of view, there are already the tools and the opportunity for a resolute re-architecture of the often horrible building heritage in the outskirts. There are a lot of examples, even directly lived, where it was possible and effective to perform an intervention using typical restoration techniques and/or small and punctual (but crucial) demolitions/replacements and/or scenarios created through overlapping facade panels, ventilated facades, new colours, architectural materials and details, and we can transform the city's appearance. Certainly the city's appearance is not the city itself or at least not only. Also there is the problem of classification of the interventions, the normative framework for facilitations and incentives, and not least, the fragmentation of property, because who exactly is the client?

19. The recovery of abandoned industrial areas in Italy has occupied a lot of space in the architectural and urban landscape of the last 25 years; can you tell us about the adventure you lived with the project of the recovery and reconversion of the Oscar Shindler factory in Krakow?

When I decided to take part in the Contest, it was not even clear from the documents of the competition that it was Oscar Schindler's factory, a bit for the Polish declination in Schindlera, a bit because in the announcement it was almost hidden and finally, because I had never been to Krakow. I was curious about the theme, the transformation of an old industrial building into a Museum of Contemporary Art, a theme that has been one of my passions forever, not just as an architect.

The factory halls, located in Zablocie's industrial and worker housing district, were abandoned and not interesting from an architectural point of view.

They had no significance, they were simply out of the way, but the municipal administration had decided to invest in culture and on this area.

In spite of the apparent collective disinterest, in the city and beyond, an ideological battle began immediately on the opportunity to allocate this place of tragic history (actually positive in the tragic historical context) to a Museum of Contemporary Art, so it would be exposed, by definition, to the "provocations of contemporary artists"; in the interviews followed in the competition and during the works, the most recurring questions were just about that topic.

Our project was born from the study of the photographic documentation that we had and the winning idea was to think of the new (requested) volumes as an extension of the existing building, an organism that, however, gradually became something completely new, strong, dynamic, contemporary, that did not hide the ancient but enhanced it, emphasising the skyline, capturing and expanding the simple and striking colours and materials, which aimed at creating a new urban context, a connective tissue more than of a building/icon, an interior exterior space, permeable, crossable, diverse and full of activities, honest, a new centre of social reality for expansion and change.

No contrast, this was the path to respect, protect, prolong and relaunch the historical and emotional content of that place into a perfect function open to the city and the world. From a practical point of view, opening a new office in Krakow was necessary in order to closely follow the design and implementation phases of the museum, an extraordinarily complex project, perhaps one of the most complex I have faced, from the technical difficulties associated with the dilapidated conditions of the old buildings, the presence of the river at a short distance, the budget and for the very short time of construction that we set ourselves (only eighteen months of construction).

20. As a designer of important concept stores, can you explain your concept of "showcase" and which elements you consider part of the public space in a city?

In 1984 the Luisa Via Roma shop opened in Florence (then they were not called concept stores); the points of reference were the American department stores, the street, the passersby drawn inside, continuing their stroll... So it was at Luisa, in fact, that we recessed the façade which made the city physically enter inside and the display window became a theatre in constant transformation, a landmark.

But then as now, the display windows ARE the street, THEY ARE the city and therefore can be beautiful or ugly, also in relation to the surroundings, the design of the shops and the windows. When it comes down to it, it is all about interior design.
I don't know when this motion will go in reverse on a large scale, but in niche and avant-garde areas, where antennas are more sensitive, something is changing rapidly.

Many star brands (e.g. Prada) no longer aim to the homologation of their image in all latitudes; in the various cities around the world, when places change, new identities are created, and even the new huge Middle East shopping malls (see Foster's project) move away from the new international style to look for a new formal vocabulary, but that also presents new behaviours.

The birth of temporary stores, stores that are born, transformed, closed, change typology, place and city in a few months, completely bypassed the belief of traditional commercial philosophy that the public is divided into levels of product or consumption. You can see things are starting to concentrate on emotions rather than on the product or the location.

21. I am very interested in the concept of Sustainable Architecture and Sustainability; Personally, I think that in particular for buildings, this concept has shifted too much to the technical aspect of the production of renewable energy, often at the expense of compositional quality. I think that we personally have to start from a culture of limiting waste and therefore consumption as civic education. What is your point of view about sustainability?

Sustainability... you can't not be part of it, but there should not be a price to pay in terms of the quality of architecture, beauty, harmony. It is equally important to reduce consumption, and it is first a philosophical choice and then a technical one, and if that is not enough, you have to decide to revise the concept of growth, perennial expansion ... Of course the reflections that fit our little ancient world should be declined in different keys when we think of Asia, Africa, etc.

22. Do you want to talk about your mutating city idea?

It is necessary to have a mutating and mutually changing architecture, less future architecture and more architecture with a future, like a story from the open end.

23. In what city would you like to live beyond Florence?

In a seaside town, Mediterranean; I would have liked to live in Naples if, twenty years ago, it had begun and continued a path similar to that which transformed Barcelona or Valencia, for example I would never want to live or have a long stay in a city without a historic and cultural identity.

Work

24. What importance does your study give to the medium of design contests?

With much passion and the awareness that it is more often than not a complete gamble, nevertheless, to get into the dimension of grand architecture, it is one of the few possible paths; beyond that, I've never gone for "dangerous relationships", politics, lobbying... and the results have come in anyway. In addition, apart from the importance of winning, the contest is almost always an interesting opportunity to deal with different themes, territories and cultures... and through that we grow.

25. Can you compare the Italian competition environment with the foreign one?

I'll say the obvious. Many competitions have very few accomplishments; many (I suppose) are based on improper, "impure" contacts, all in play before, during and after; also everything is conditioned too much by the style of the moment... Abroad it isn't any easier. Some countries, like France, seem in lock down; others are difficult considering our background, e.g. Germany, England, but the opportunities are many; we fished out the joker with Poland (two big competitions won) seven years ago because at that stage Poland was not very considered.

26. Which of your competition projects would you like to be built?

Thought and unrealised? (Consiag Prato, 1st; Abu Dhabi Stadium; MACRO, 4th; Chamber of Commerce, 4th; Scicli, 2nd; Tarquinia Airport...) or not yet thought of but that is part of the wishes? I would love to do a grand set design for the theatre.

27. When you approach a competition project, do you let yourself be guided by your idea of the project and then develop the programme or is the program considered from the start to be the guide to follow?
The project for a competition is no different from any other project, except that the client judges us, all a fast process. Then the commission; the ability to astonish becomes of greater value, more than it would be acceptable or not. However the approach is the same, instinctive and therefore the idea and maybe we should say the vision guides us; then follows all the professional verification work: that the idea works, meets all the requirements, the competition guidelines and the expectations?

28. How do you consider the research and work

of Claudio Nardi Architects in relation to the international architectural panorama?

Atypical because it tries to avoid labels; varies, tries, tries, fails, works in the small and the big without snobbism, and often avoids those opportunities of communication and presence in the places that count.

29. I am personally fond of biographies, starting from the assumption that a great project always stems from a great relationship between architect and contractor; I think of L. Kahn and Jonas Salk, rather than Wright and Herbert Johnson; can you tell us about your experience?

As I always say the client is the project; when there is no client or the client is "absent", one feels that absence and I have to invent an alter ego with whom to discuss it, to make it grow.

30. What relationship do you have with the construction site ?

We need to take a step back; I don't have all the know how and maybe it's a widespread problem, to produce excellent detailed projects that combine sensibility and beauty with efficiency, innovation, budget... I've learned everything in small and large worksites empirically, and so my relationship with the site (almost always in the artistic direction and almost never in construction management), even on large projects, is an organism that grows, transforms, which can improve, correcting mistakes, a passionate relationship but perhaps not aligned with the production standards of the building industry, which is why I always try to collaborate with professionals in the executive phase, constantly following the path... it is the beginning of the construction site.

31. What do you think about Italy at this time? Can it always be a good place for an architect?

It could be, but the space of greater manoeuvre is not in the opportunity of transforming new territories and anyway, when it happens, I would like to see a new, original language, a product of our culture, not inspired by google search. I can't stand architecture based on successful models applied anywhere and everywhere.

32. In your interviews you often talk about "level duality", near - distant, big - small; can you explain this particular point of view?

I started on my own and from small projects, creating for everyday life; from interior design came the path that was gradually enriched and enlarged to include everything that was possible to design. Ambitious interiors, architecture at various scales, design, cultivating the aspiration that every project left glimpses of the elements of the path, the formula, the intentions, the doubles... so that the work had at last so many levels of reading, like the books I love most.

Three questions that I particularly care about.

33. Who is the Architect for you? What role do you have in society? What contribution should one bring?

The role of the architect has always been a fundamental role, and today the mission should be to protect us from ourselves, from laziness, from greed, disinterest, and from an addiction to ugliness.

34. What does creating architecture mean to you?

It means acting in a very profound and very risky manner in the space we inhabit; it is a continuous transformation. In reality the architect's gesture is severely underestimated in respect to other gestures far more in the eyes of the public: they are all astonished at the advertising and multimedia communications because through the image they think there maybe a risky intervention that depends on the type of message about society. In fact, even the ugly buildings or anonymous buildings that are apparently underestimated have a very heavy negative force, and in the opposite, the wonderful architecture, something that, in addition to being beautiful and communicative, has a tremendous effect on the path to achieving happiness. It's a job I consider very important and very difficult, which I do with great passion and desire.

35. What would you recommend to a young architect at the beginning of his career?

Not to give up, not to be in a hurry and not to hunger for success; the market today accepts everything, but it's better to grow slowly and through experiences, even small, but direct, tangible; know and converse with the client, frequent artisans, and learn from them at least as much you learn from the fantastic and fast technological evolution we know through the web.

Try not to be self-referential, which is the temptation of architects and therefore also of young architects who feel they have to tell the story their way; it is right to make a tale for themselves and for others. Learn not to use all the ideas that come to mind and not all together. According to me in each project there is a fundamental idea and then many ideas that are the materials, shapes, details that join the recognisable founding idea and then the path leading to a happy result is the subtraction of the signs. Do not leave them all; that is a mistake that often even the big names do; so at the base of everything there's a kind of refining self-control at the end and next to this there's fantasy, watching and learning, like learning to read in order to write. If one does not learn to look, he does not learn to look at everything, from the great architectures in the past, to the small, the smallest, the anonymous, the objects of everyday use, innovation; information and curiosity are paramount! One needs enormous baggage and then you find yourself in front of a space where you need an idea that shortcircuits everything; it is not done by sketching at a table; I think in front of every project there is a solution when we have all the information and a shortcircuiting idea. Then maybe it takes a year to fix it, but it's only a minute for the idea; but as long as there is no shortcircuit it is very difficult to come up with something good afterwards, even having worked a long time.

CLAUDIO NARDI

Claudio Nardi, architect, born in Prato on 3/9/1951.

He produces architectural projects, for public and private clients, in Italy and, above all, abroad. Amongst the most recent works : museum buildings for Mu.Ca. (Museum of Shipbuilding) in Monfalcone and for MOCAK (Museum of Contemporary Art of Krakow, former Schindler Factory) in Krakow, office buildings for Mandragora Headquarters in Florence, the new headquarters of the Port Authority in Marina di Carrara, Vertex Tower and Office Building in Amman, new Town Hall offices in Krakow, residential and tourist venues such as Apartment Building and Riva Lofts in Florence; recently also the set-up Bridge of Love on the Arno river in Florence.

Among the private designs, various residences in Beijing, Parma, Madrid, Tel Aviv, Rome, Marina di Pietrasanta and Civitanova Marche. Among his many projects in the fashion world there are names like Dolce & Gabbana, Ferrè, Valentino, Malo, Hogan and concept stores in Hanoi, Saigon, Florence (Luisa Via Roma), Rome and Guangzhou. He deals often with the theme of transformation, the relationship between innovation and history, between form and function, between "product" and communication.

Every time, his work involves in-depth study, not only in his own sphere of specialisation; every project, even an interior, is to a large extent developed through the use of light, sensitive materials and particular combinations of surfaces, volumes, solids and open space.

The roots of a language that is constantly enriched with new expressions can be found in Mediterranean culture and Italian rationalism, but constant experimentation and the experience of new materials and technologies, new and ancient sites, have enabled Nardi to develop innovative themes and functions. In this view, the themes of large-scale architecture, of residential or commercial space, of art exhibition, all have equal importance and create an interior continuum of active, harmonious transferral of knowledge.

Among other activities: he teaches at the Department of Architecture in Florence and gives lectures in various spheres.

He has won many prizes and awards in architectural exhibitions and competitions including:

Academic correspondent for the Academy of Drawing Arts, Florence, Italy, 2014.
Professional Recognition for Architecture – Rotary Club, Florence, Italy, 2013.
Platinum Drill, Prize for Public Building, Warsaw, Poland, 2013 MOCAK.
2013 Mies van der Rohe Award-Nomination, Barcelona, Spain, 2013 MOCAK.
Idea-Tops, International Space Design Award, Shenzhen, China, 2012 MOCAK.
European Prize of Architecture Philippe Rotthier, Brussels, Belgium, 2011 MOCAK.
International Biennal "Barbara Capocchin" Prize for Architecture, Padova, Italy, 2011 MOCAK.
International Prize Dedalo Minosse to the Client in Architecture, Vicenza, Itally, 2011 MOCAK.
Wallpaper International Awards, First Place Best New Hotel, Florence, Italy, 2008 Riva Lofts Hotel.
Hotel & Lodge Prize, Awarded Hotel Contest

Florence, Italy, 2008 Riva Lofts Hotel.

D&D Awards, Best Kitchen System, London, UK, 2004 Bianca Kitchen.

Architectural Prize "Città di Oderzo", Oderzo, Italy, 2001 Five Villas in Lignano Sabbiadoro.

V Biennial Exhibition of Architecture, Marcello D'Olivo Award, Pordenone, Italy, 1999 Five Villas in Lignano Sabbiadoro.

Architecture Competitions

Czartoryski Museum Interiors, Kraków, Poland, 2017 - Competition, Second Place.

Fredry Publishing House, Warsaw, Poland, 2017 – Competition, Third Place.

Mu.Ca Museum of Shipbuilding, former Hotel Workers, Monfalcone, Italy, 2012 - Competition, First Place.

New Town Hall, Krakow, Poland, 2008 - Competition, First Place.

MOCAK, former Oscar Schindler's Factory, Krakow, Poland, 2007 - Competition, First Place.

Port Autority, Marina di Carrara, Italy, 2006 - Competition, First Place.

Ideas competition for the redevelopment of the ex"SAICA", Porto di Alghero, Sassari, Italy, 2005 – Third Place.

Competition for the redevolopment and expansion of the professional institute for hotel services, Tortolì, Nuoro, Italy, 2004 – Second Place.

International ideas competition of the Waterfront Lignano Sabbiadoro, Udine, Italy, 2002 - First Place.

Covered Grand-Stand, Sporting Club, Abu Dhabi, U.A.E., 2001- Competition upon invitation.

Redesign of Piazza Matteotti, Tavarnelle Val di Pesa, Italy, 2002 - Competition, First Place.

Consiag New Headquarters, Prato, Italy, 1999 - First Place, Second Stage.

Biography

1970 Interior Design consultant for Poltronova, Florence.

1971 Interior Design consultant at Design Centre, Florence.

1973-1974 Collaboration with Carlo Scarpa to the planning of the International Design, Florence.

1973- 1977 Interior Design consultant at Design Centre, Florence.

1978 Master's Degree at the Department of Architecture in Florence.

1978 Foundation of the Studio "Claudio Nardi Architetto".

18-05-1979 License to practice at Order of Architects in Florence.

2002/2005 and 2006/2008 Teaching at the Department of Architecture in Florence.

2005/2006 Teaching at the Kent State University in Florence.

2007 Opening of the office in Krakow.

2008 License to practice at Order of Architects in Poland.

2010 Founding Member of EX3, Centre for the Contemporary Art in Florence.

TALES

Claudio Nardi Studio, Florence, Italy, 2005

Temporary Installation "Bridge of Love" Florence, Italy, 2016

Beauty that is ethereal but yet tangible, emotional and habitable, both to one's touch and one's sight. White clouds lying on the waters' surface, traversed by mist and perfume, by the light of early dawn until the sunset, caressed by breezes and sounds.

Throughout the history of the city, the river has been everything, and now it is a Non-Place that, for the first time hosts an emerging life, becoming a Place to stay, an experience of a new and surprising view of the city, its very heart. It becomes again the centre, the main character, observed through its transparent walls alternating between being the stage and the audience at the same time.

The idea of the floating pavilions comes from the historically established tradition that has been lost in the passage of time – one of floating pontoons on the river hosting small cafés. Those small lounges, rooms even, made the river a vivid element of the social life of the city. Design intent was to bring back to this tradition and to propose the river once again a part of the city. The temporary installation was part of the events organised for the Pitti fashion week in 2016.

A palace of nine pavilions connected by passages and narrow bridges, nine floating living rooms, positioned, like white, transparent, theatrical boxes, floating on the surface of the river, scene of a magical candlelight dinner, and, during the following days, many different events and exhibitions.

Temporary Installation "Aria", Florence, Italy, 2017

Temporary Pavilions on the bastions of the Belvedere Fort.

The inflatable pavilions in taut and transparent PVC,
are placed on the ground and overlook Florence. Large
transparent bubbles, linked together, like clouds,
habitable clouds, which will host exhibitions, events,
theatre, and music.

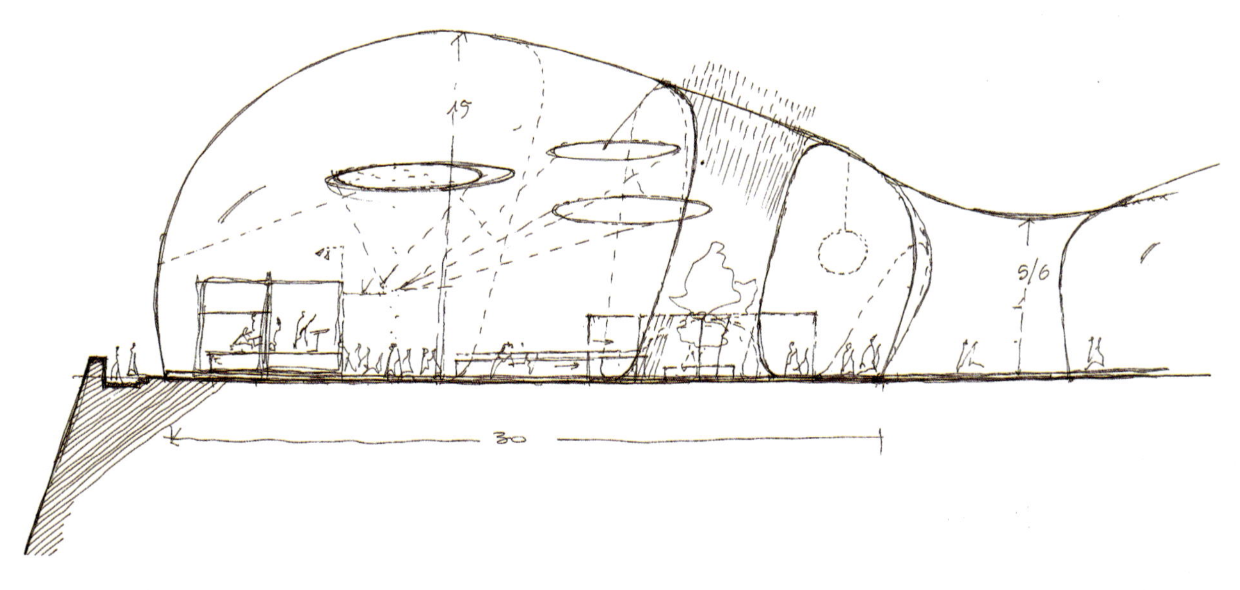

FASHION

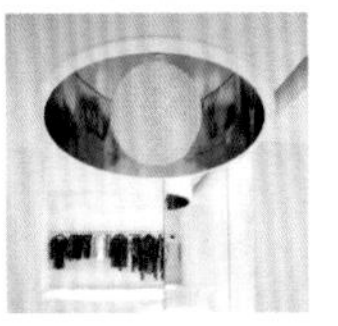

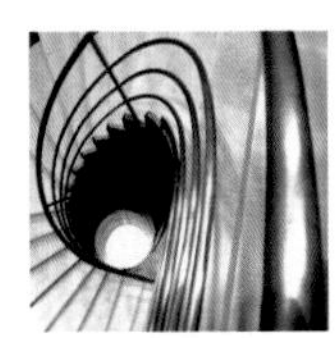

Concept Store Luisa Via Roma, Florence, Italy, 1984

Concept Store Luisa Via Roma, Florence, Italy, 2008

A project of grand simplistic formality, yet at the same time radical in the choice of its content: the diaphanous light of thick glass and the impenetrable mass of concrete.

A space apparently nude yet subtle sophisticated, a Baroque scenography stripped of decoration, pulsating, constantly interacting with the light of the seasons and human sensations.

The hard clear light of morning translated by the LED lighting system which diffused throughout the store gives a sense of a perennial dawn.

A non-static space which mutates, an articulated composition, almost becoming an outdoor world, simultaneously natural and artificial, the marriage of invention and mirage.

044

Concept Store Luisa Via Roma, Prato, Italy, 2002

Dior
ALESSANDRO DELL'ACQUA

Sbaiz Fashion Store, Lignano Sabbiadoro, Italy, 1988

Boutique Clara Lorj, Florence, Italy, 2009

DOLCE GABBANA

Boutique Dolce & Gabbana, Milan, Italy, 1988 - 1995

The unadorned palace, remote memories for a new grandeur.

"The space is developed on the classical proportions of an aristocratic and bourgeois living room, where pigments and oxides that, without melting, have stratified onto the walls, exuding the many tales of the palace. The southern light bursts through the large framed window; the exterior is dazzling and the interior of memories blends in without losing themselves. I thought of these spaces as Italian songs, filled with feelings, traditions and passions. The environment is divided into two parts; from the openings that separate them, a bright light flares in, as if, suddenly, in the large dark room (which is the first environment) someone has opened the shutters, giving free range to the blinding power of a Mediterranean sun. The floor, symbol of an ancient craftsmanship, reminiscent of a past measure of time, feeling and luxury. The slabs of the floor, in slate and grey marble, are hand engraved and decorated with scagliola, according to the artisan tradition still common in Italy, reproducing an ancient Gothic design, a powerful representation of rampant lions."

Boutique Malo, Milan, Italy, 2000 and Roma, Italy, 2001

A concept for the realm of cashmere, of hugging warmth,
was imagined through the combination of rooms, lines
and materials of domestic inspiration, in a declination of
cool colors that even more exalts the tactile warmth of the
protagonist material.

Boutique Dina, Arezzo, Italy, 2009

Boutique Atil Kutoglu, Istanbul, Turkey, 2009

The Atil Kutoglu (Turkish fashion designer working in Europe) concept store tells the contamination between two worlds, East and West. Bright and contemporary atmospheres, modern and sophisticated furnishings, objects join decorative elements and the re-interpretations of Ottoman culture, opulent and mysterious.

Hanoi, we are on the border of a perfumed and messy
world and here is the western touch of crystal as the
material that separates, which emphasizes, exhibits and
organizes the display spaces and boxes, within a light
texture made of rich, tactile, decorated materials.

Boutique Beayukmui, Florence, Italy, 2011

An abstract room suspended in a drawn world, fantastic and poetic.

A dialogue between two substances, the rational and geometric one with the functional and the oneiric one, told by the complex design that reproduces fantastic birds on the ceiling, on the walls, on the floor, everywhere.

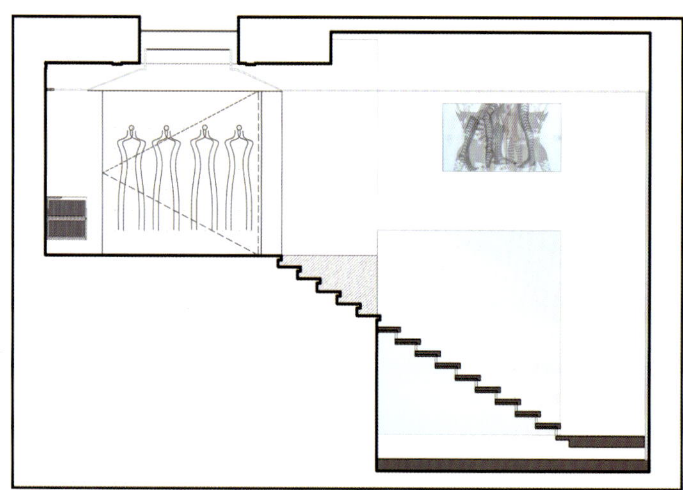

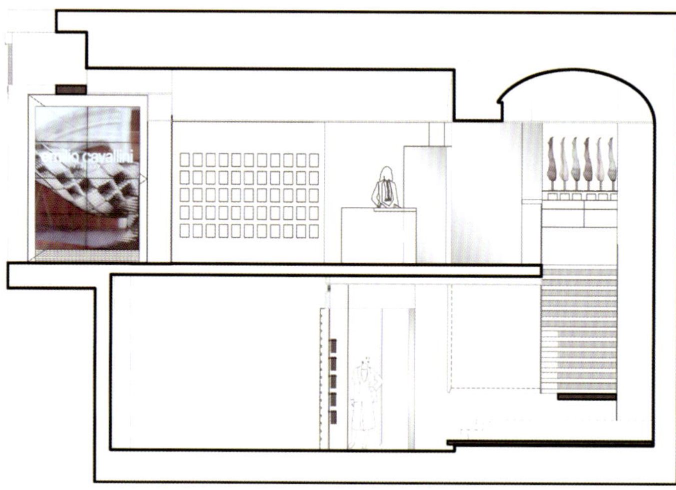

Boutique Emilio Cavallini, Florence, Italy, 2012

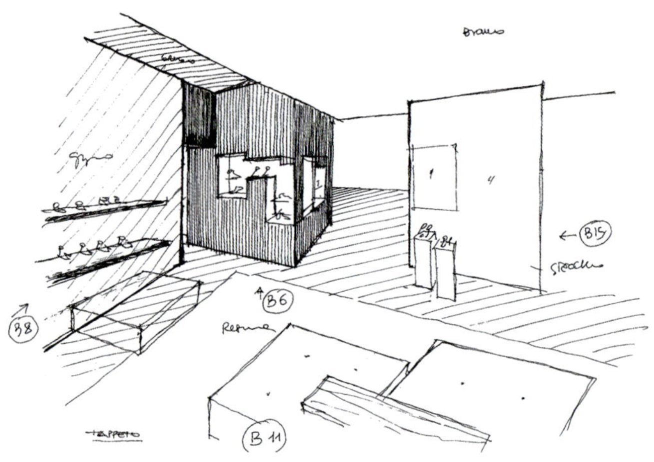

Boutique Strategia, Milan, Italy, 2015

The boutique is situated in a large square and the internal space can be seen through four geometrical and irregular "windows" and it continues indoors, simple and concrete. The decorated walls are gently excavated by irregular and almost natural niches, framed by the lines of burnished metal. That niches create exhibit surfaces at different levels and depths like miniature theatres, with changing scenarios.

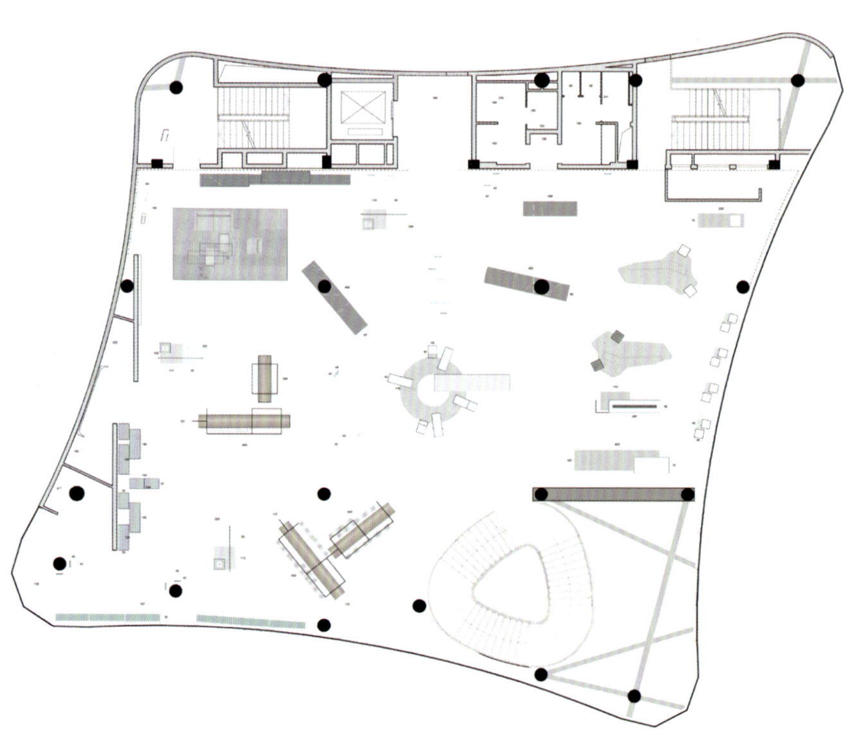

Modern Avenue Concept Store, Project, Guangzhou, China, 2016

SPACES

———

VOLTI DI MARMO

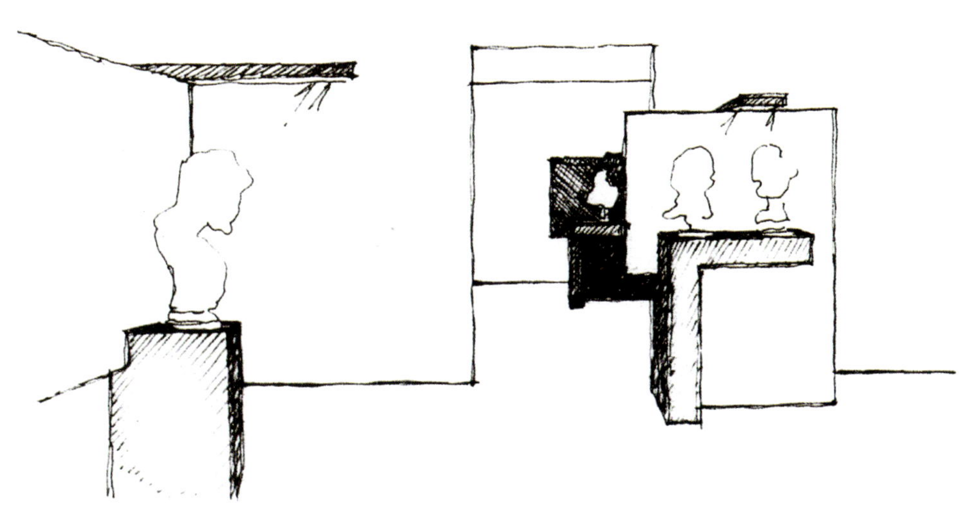

Marble Heads Exhibition, Florence, Italy, 2001

The displays integrate the busts and heads without diminishing their singularity: they become their expressive extension in space disappearing and nullifying in it.

The use of various possible exhibition themes (bases, panels, lighting) has created an "exhibition element" that is not just a new object, but an experience. The shapes, techniques and materials used for the displays offer themselves in apparent service to the exposed objects and with their knowledge. Their properties, called to exhibit and develop the properties of the exposed objects, actually they define them and remain defined. By interacting, they constitute a meaningful structure, an experience of knowledge.

079

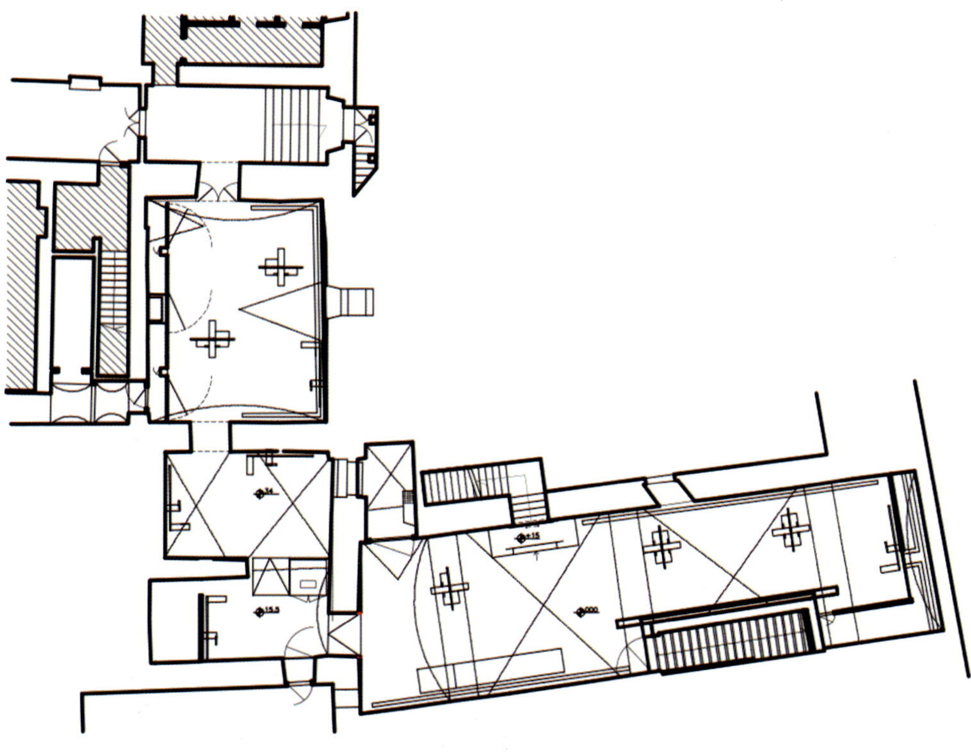

Marble Museum, Florence, Italy, 2006

Showroom ZR, Florence, Italy, 2006

The project plays on black and white dualism, shadow
and light, transparency and matter, to create a theatrical
environment and emotional impact, a space open to
multiple transformations, extactly like a teather.

Showroom Arketipo, Florence, Italy, 2006

Mandragora Bookshop Agora|Z, Palazzo Strozzi, Florence, Italy, 2009

Mandragora Bookshop Battistero, Florence, Italy, 2008

museo cantieris
musca

ICA MONFALCONE

Museum of Shipbuilding, Competition, First Prize, Monfalcone, Italy, 2017

MU-Ca, The Museum of Shipbuilding in Monfalcone, was created through a complete transformation of the pre-existing complex and with an interior design for exhibitions. The Museum tells the story of the site and the city in an exhibition itinerary divided into sections, through testimonies and documents of over a century of history, using a contemporary and light touch joined with a multimedia language.

Riva Lofts, Wallpaper Awards 2008: Best New Hotel, Florence, Italy, 2007

Halfway between being at home and halfway between being away, these lofts are testimonials and participants in contemporary living yet also travel experiences through time and space. This group of buildings, which looks rather like a small country hamlet in the Tuscan countryside, was a small factory in 1880, later transformed into artisan workshops and then in 2006 into "a home for guests". Ten suites are conceived in the style of French studios, blending a metropolitan lifestyle with the welcoming and domestic atmosphere. Fusion is the leading theme behind the structure's conception: pure and contemporary, the warm atmosphere in these distinctive spaces is due to a series of recovered historic elements – modern antiques (1950's furniture), old and new materials (wood and corian) – and examples of sophisticated design.

Thus the suites, interiors, all distinctly unique in size, shape and arrangement, boast a well-defined and recognisable character. They also offer a series of different perceptions of the environment thanks to the possibility of choosing between a suite with a private terrace, a suite directly overlooking the garden, or offering panoramic views either over the Cascine Park or towards Brunelleschi's Cupola.

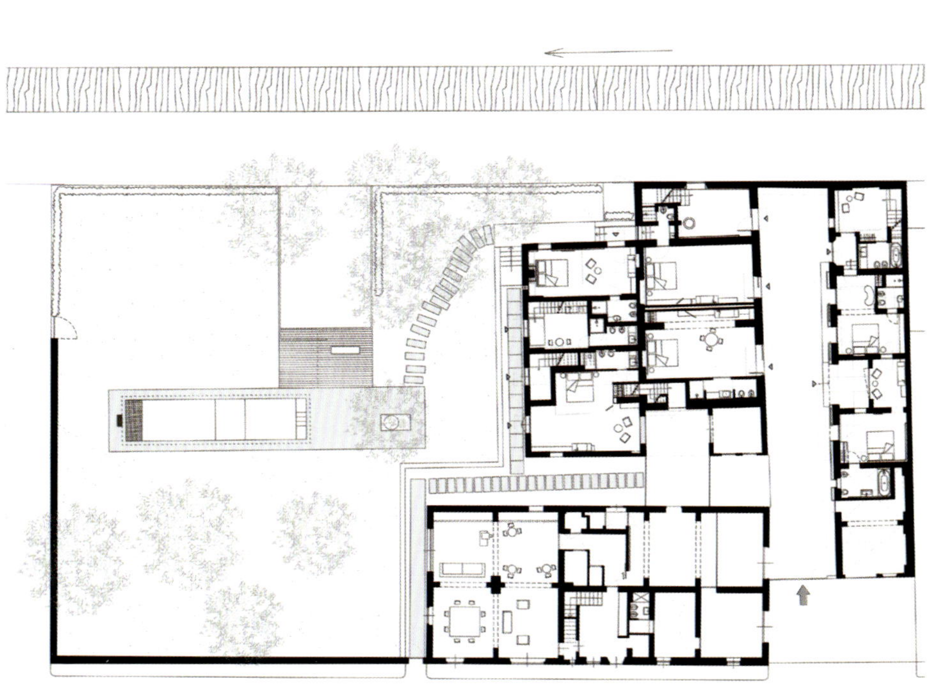

C2 Contemporary Art Gallery, Florence, Italy, 2016

A simple and neutral space, a place where art seems to
be born where everything is possible.

C3 LAB, Florence, Italy, 2016

This is a multifunctional space: workshop, theatre and exhibition space.

The service functions are integrated at a reduced level, so as to leave the perception and continuity of the environment untouched at times.

Porcinai Showroom, Fiesole, Italy, 2009

It was the atelier of Pietro Porcinai, great landscape
architect, became now a contemporary and metropolitan
space, full of traces of travel, nature and knowledge, a
space vibrating of natural light and mutable in different
geometries .

Villa Romana Pavillon, Florence, Italy, 2017

The pavilion is sited in the garden of Villa Romana – a neoclassical building, which in 1905 became the oldest German residence for artists based abroad – and used for interdisciplinary events organised by the foundation Villa Romena.

The garden and the pavilion are opened up as a space for exercise and perception and as a venue for talks and activities.

Wine and Cigar Bar, Beijing, China, 2017, Work in Progress

雪茄吧

Creating an elegant and luxurious contemporary wine and cigar bar and cellar involved the development of an idea where materials and forms recreated the essence of the exclusive wine experience combined with a relaxed private club.

In the cellar room the use of dark stone walls and floor with curved ceilings surfaced with wood print evokes an underground cellar atmosphere with the two long refrigerated walls that accentuate the bottles floating in light. Repeating oak wine rack units designed in simple elegance continue the traditional cellar feel adding also the sense of a private wine collection.

The Wine Bar is contained by two slightly curved walls, faced in oak wood, reminiscent of a Barrique. Screened off by two semi-transparent sliding doors to the entrance and by curtains towards the outside terrace. It is furnished with a brass service desk with stools and two sitting rooms with armchairs and tables for tasting.

The Cigar Lounge is imagined as a large room of a modern gentleman's club, comfortable, relaxed, with carpets, a feature wall bookcase with books, objects and paintings, ethanol fireplaces, soft lights, armchairs and sofas. The room opens out into the furnished outdoor terrace with its teak flooring and planters.

Czartoryski Museum Interiors, Competition, Second Prize, Krakow, Poland, 2017

Isolation of the exquisite.

The Czartoryskich Museum is the oldest museum in Poland. It consists of two exposures – one related to the history of Poland and the other of Western European art. The actual historic building of the museum is a precious envelope that needs to become contemporary in order to highlight and enhance the museum experience of the works of art and historical artifacts. The challenge lay in creating a new connecting aesthetic between the two collections exhibited within the same environment.

The feature element of the project is the design of the Leonardo Room, dedicated to Leonardo da Vinci's painting "Lady with an Ermine". The idea was to create a suspended, abstract, virtual context, a perfect geometry in the asymmetrical and trapezoidal space of the room. A solid screen, aligned with the geometry of the skylight and suspended from the ground and ceiling, is a frame and contains the work in a dedicated, illuminated and protected space, isolating it from the context.

RESIDENTIAL

114

Seafront Villa, Shelter Island, NY, USA, 1999

A residence by the sea. The villa on the water is a
contemporary home in which architecture meets design
and the taste of simplicity, through the experimentation of
a constructive language typical of the American tradition.

Villa Sant'Ilario, Tuscany, Italy, 1999

The exterior has the spare charm of a country house. The interior has the communicative force of clear gestures, spaces, and light. In the hills of Tuscany, an imposing late-18th century house takes on a new identity. The design intervention is decisive in the interiors, creating an absolutely contemporary atmosphere. The rooms are arranged to permit the members of the family to enjoy a certain degree of autonomy, but with many opportunities for socialising and conversation. The regular, symmetrical layout is organised around a new central two-storey space, faced by an access balcony, creating a greater sense of space. The linearity of the layout is attenuated by theatrical lighting effects: natural zenithal light penetrates through a series of eight skylights; the design of the skylights is also reflected in the arrangement of the lighting fixtures. Outside, a large plaza, paved in stone, offers a space for outdoor living, enhancing the image of the main façade.

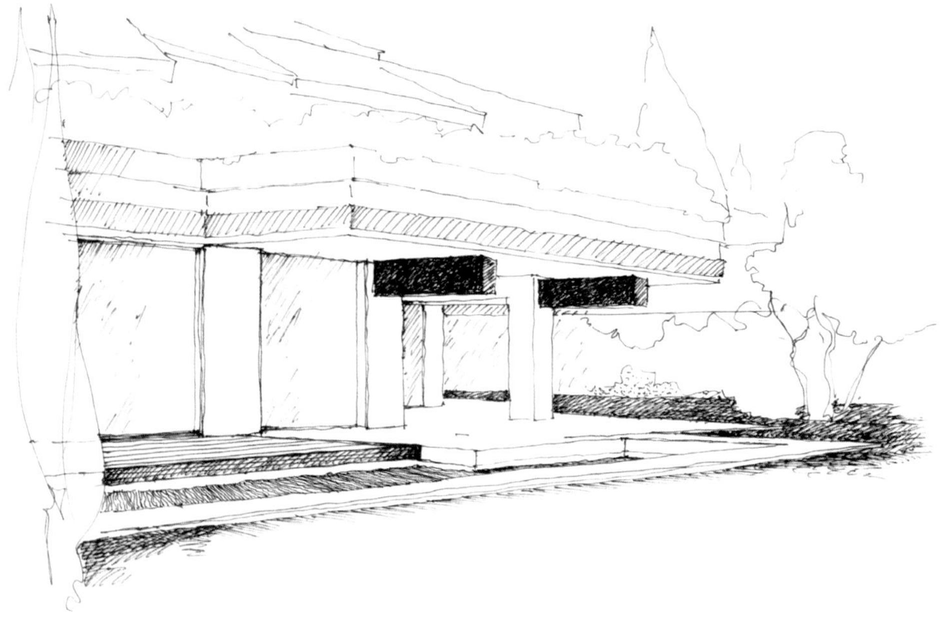

Villa, Florence, Italy, 2002

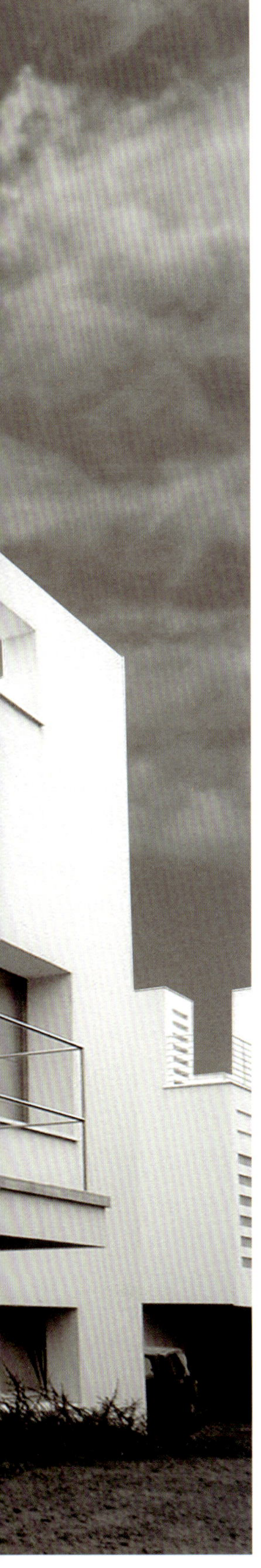

Residential Complex, Lignano Sabbiadoro, Italy, 1997
Marcello D'Olivo Prize, 1999
Oderzo City Architectural Prize, 2001

Ancient concepts redefined for the modern necessity of privacy.

Each home develops around its centre, an inner courtyard where the main façades and the entrance area converge into a stopover and meeting point. The large central open-air "room" is designed to accommodate intimacy and create privacy with respect to the neighbours and adjoining buildings. It is a clear and direct inspiration to the traditional plans of the Arabian and subsequently Mediterranean houses. Once the large sliding glass windows are opened, a system of reciprocal relations are established between the rooms circling around the court. A large teak sliding shutter encloses or draws out this vital space to the outdoors. The upper floor follows the courtyard's perimetre masonry housing the sleeping areas and a large sun terrace. The "C" shape allows the exposure of almost all environments to the south. All materials used, from lime-based plaster to sandstone, the articulation of façades, light colours and teak shutters result from the search for material that is sensitive to vibration and changes in natural light. The development is designed with each home having its own well-defined green space. The introduction of tall trees and hedges has been studied to ensure greater privacy and the identification of the paths inside the development.

123

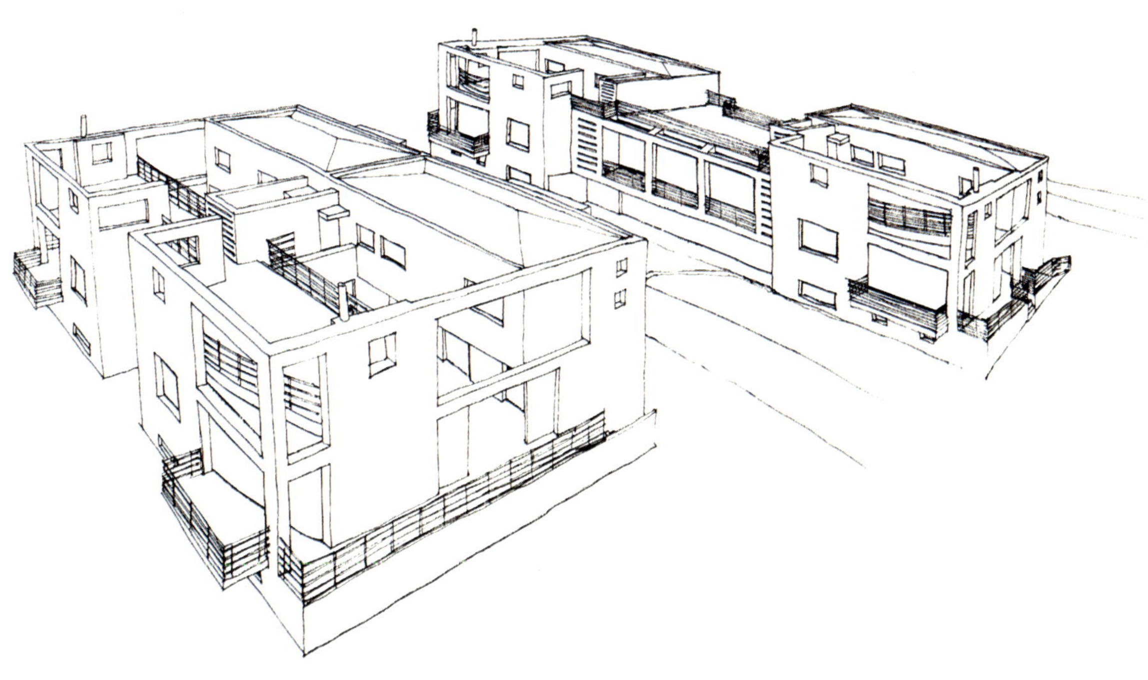

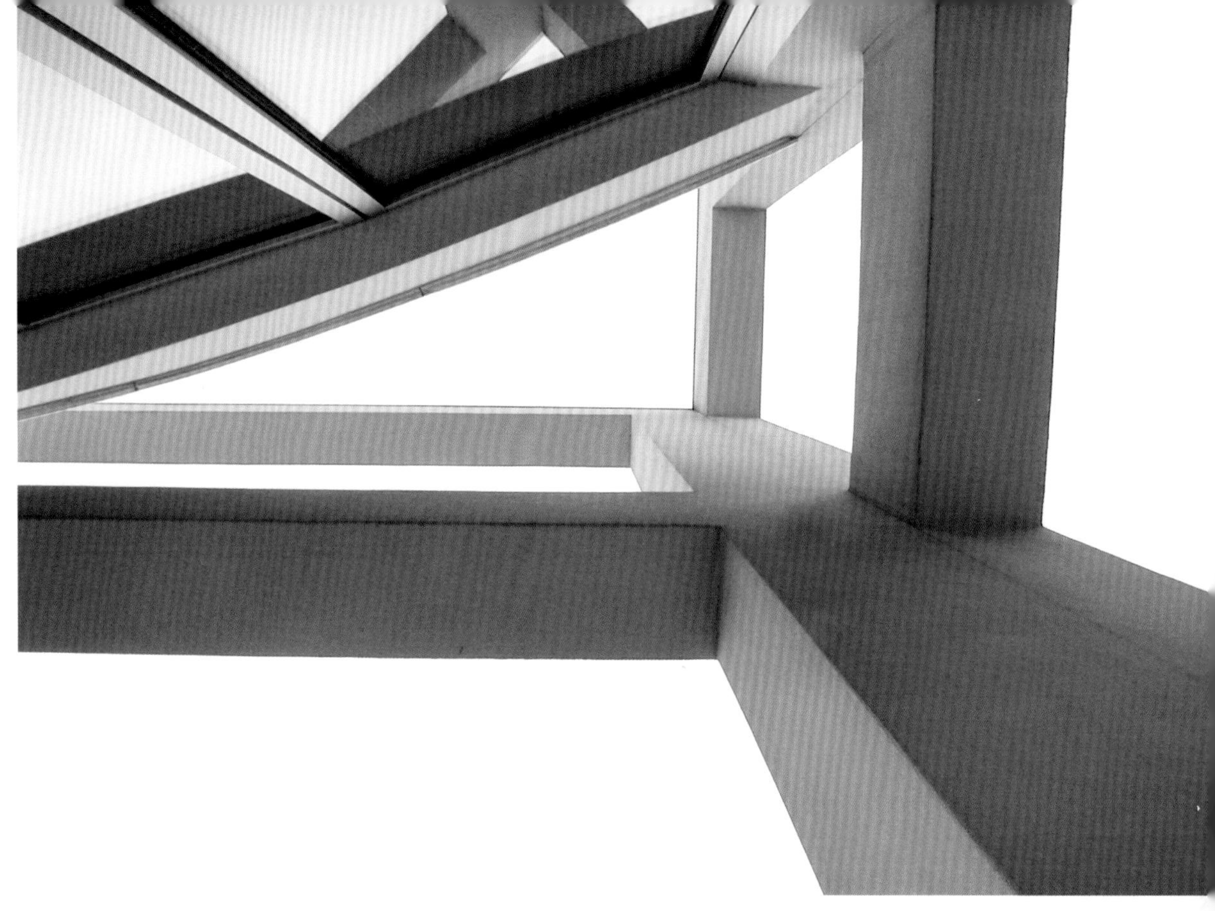

Private House, Tel Aviv, Israel, 2016

Located in the district of Neve Zedek, the oldest in Tel
Aviv, the existing building has been the subject of a
complete redesign, with a passionate Mediterranean
inspiration, through the disclosure of the main spaces
of the ground floor to the intimate atmosphere of
the private inner courtyard which, with its silent
pool, becomes the protagonist of the house. The
interior spaces are arranged at various levels and are
connected to one another, also visually, through a
large double-height void above the living room.

Private House, Madrid, Spain, 2006

A home in the sky.

Almost a work of urban transformation: from a messy array of small spaces and additions to the top floor of a 1960s building in the centre of Madrid into a large, luminous loft space. A penthouse that conveys the rationalist alphabet of the building, extending it to the outside and to the sky through the large south-facing glass windows (shaded by stainless steel mesh slides) and the small secret courtyard at the centre of the house. This 300 m² apartment project was entirely entrusted to the taste of Claudio Nardi, who not only took charge of the renovation work but also created the interior design and selected the furnishings.

Lofts Via Ghibellina, Florence, Italy, 2006

Re-architecture, transforming a factory into lofts.

The concept was to expose and enhance the soul of the building without suffocating it with extensive renovations.

The existing building (ex-factory) was transformed in three distinct living units, two of which are symmetrical with one another. Merging the two units together created the large open common space where natural light acquires a crucial role in enhancing the sophisticated colour scheme of shades from white to pearl grey and in highlighting the rare elegant signs of architectural composition.

Besides paying homage to the Italian Rationalist

Architecture, these signs leave some of the pre-existing building architectural features visible, like the saw-tooth roof with the large windows of the two symmetrical lofts and the reinforced concrete structure.

The first two living units are divided by a longitudinal wall and in both of them, the main rooms are planned on two levels, creating a large day-time area on the ground floor and a night-time area on the intermediate floor. The top floor is occupied by a single living unit, which is designed as a unique space, leading to two terraces overlooking the saw-tooth roof and connected to the ground floor by a sky-lighted staircase.

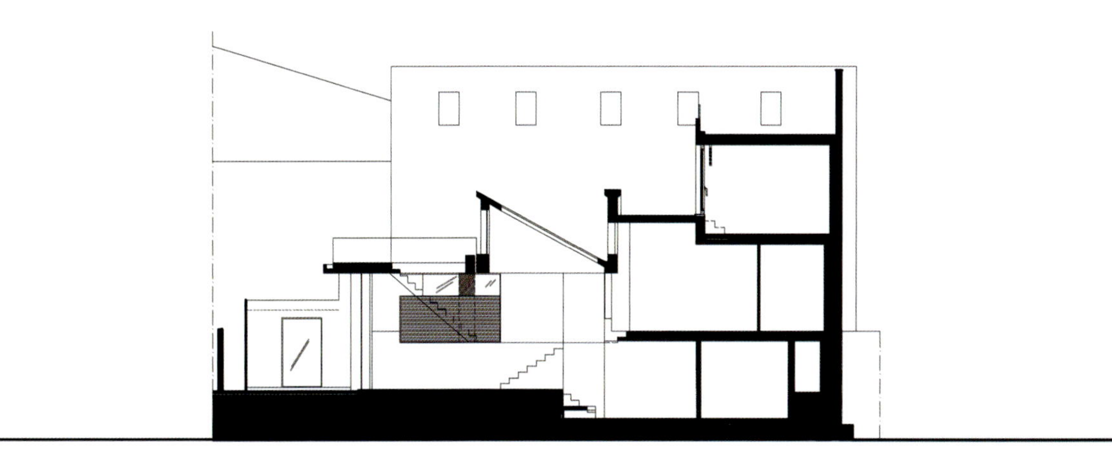

Atelier House, Florence, Italy, 2012

Conversion of an old ceramics factory into a residence.

The creation of a new dynamic flowing space from a confusing network of small rooms with a new empty space carved out of the centre – an internal courtyard, the new heart of the home in the Mediterranean tradition. The dramatic exterior volumes are enhanced by the strong red plasterwork which reflects into the interiors. Articulated spaces lead to the centralised living/activity area of the kitchen, dining and entertaining area with its fireplace. The combination of warm neutral colours and materials, the varying ceiling heights and materials mutate into a timeless decor.

Villa Aemilia, Parma, Italy, 2010

This is the encounter between a recent building (but in neoclassical style) with some modern, light architecture, made of transparencies; interior spaces that, without interruption, visually intersect with nature and with the garden, or rather the gardens, obtained at various levels, including the basement overlooking the new small lowered courtyard.

The house greatly increases its surfaces, downwards and outwards, a light and transparent volume, extruded, overlooking the valley and cantilevering on the garden, in a dialogue for contrasts with the calm design of the existing façade.

Toscoquattro, Collections: "Opera", "Concerto", "Chorus", 2004 - 2010

Forms of nature conjugated to absolute forms, abstract, technological materials combined with those of ancient and precious essences.

The bathroom acts the role of "room", no more a service space, but the centre of a "new domestic landscape". Who would call the bathroom today only a "service area"?

The bathroom which has always been an area remote from the activity centres of the home now redefines itself in the role of the environment of well-being, of the care of the person, of relaxation, in that which is apparently an evolution, but which is in fact revealed, a recovery of traditions already present in our past history in Western and Eastern cultures.

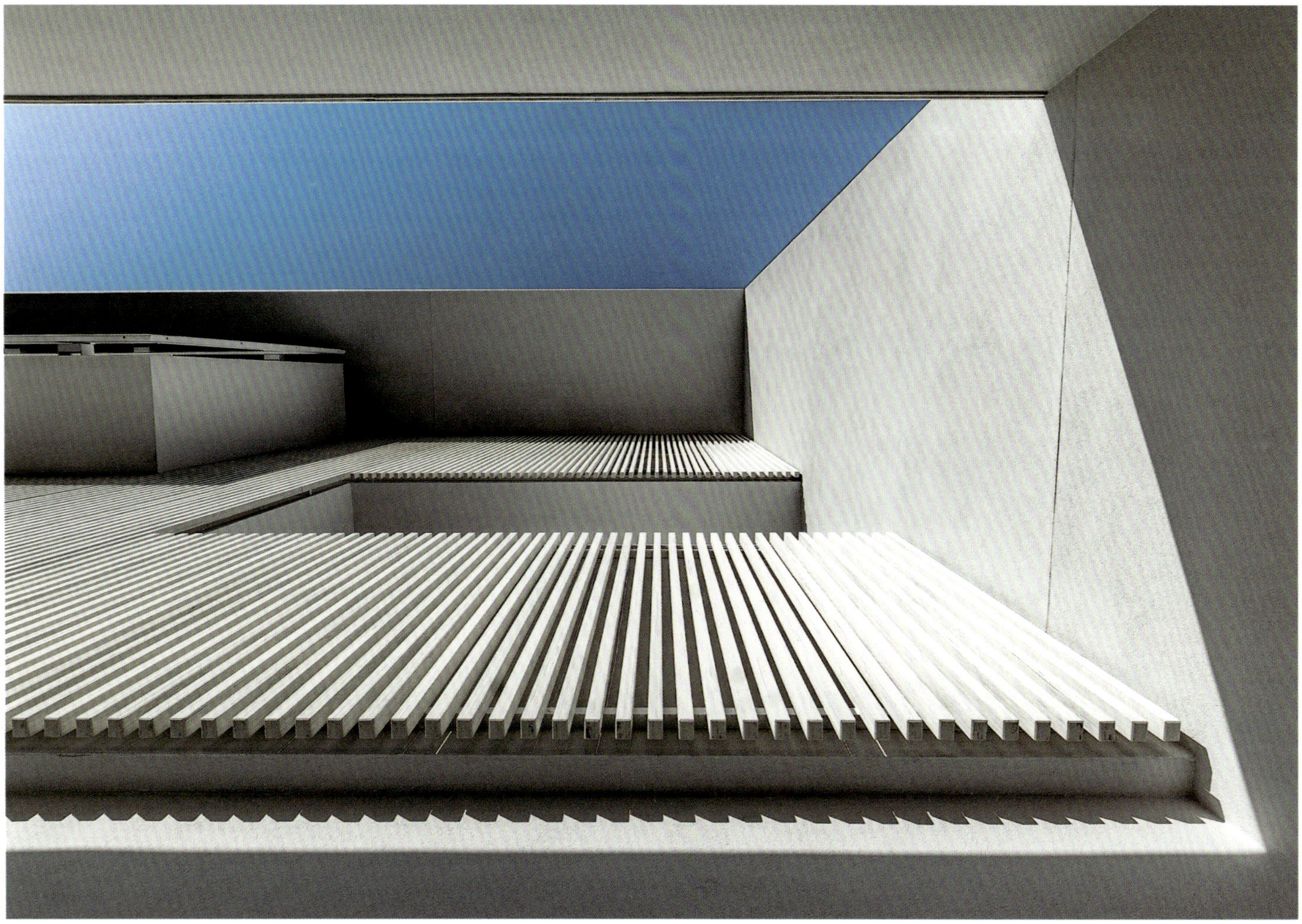

Villa Iachi, Civitanova Marche, Italy, 2017

The villa on four levels appears to always have been like this, but instead it is all a transformation, the departure from the preexisting outline, somewhat complicated, seeming to want to escape the needs of the place and its functions (that of a single house). For this the existing profile has been enclosed like being in a nautilus shell, made up of solid volumes, of opening windows and fixed glazing, of terraces and absolute empty voids, like an 18th century dress; a form that doesn't neccessarily respect the content.

A round house that closes internally open spaces, connected by a staircase that wants to be a decorative element rather than an architectural one, which interacts on all the different levels instead of being a confining factor and becomes the intergrating element of the interior.

Villa Al Manara, Dubai, U.A.E., 2008

Villa Jumeirah Palm, Dubai, U.A.E., 2014

Villa, Dubai, U.A.E., 2014

Villa, Dubai, U.A.E., 2009

168

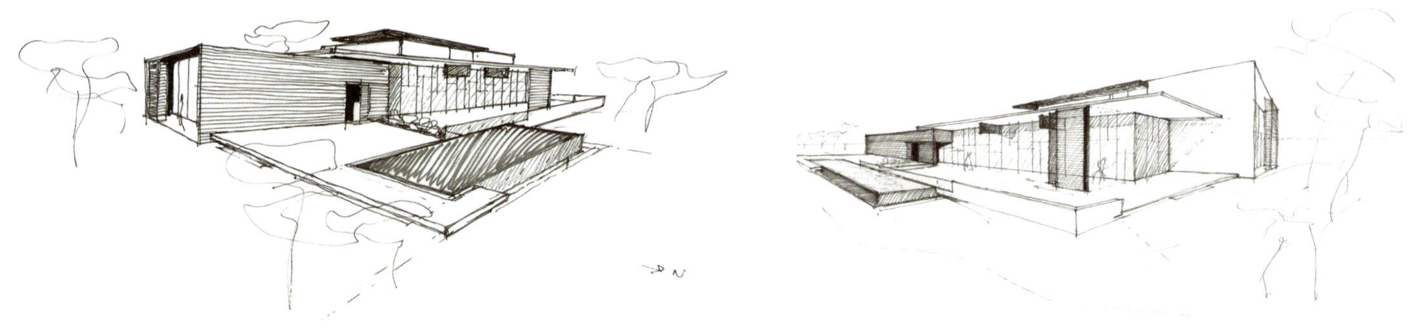

Villa Australia, Scone, Australia, 2016

A house made of lightness, horizontal surfaces that touch each other, large openings and solid blocks (rammed earth) that anchor to the Australian red earth a system of shaded and open rooms. The rooms are aggregated around the inner courtyard (Mediterranean inspiration), or facing, all around, towards the boundless landscape and the pool.

Villa Belvedere, Tuscany, Italy, Work in Progress

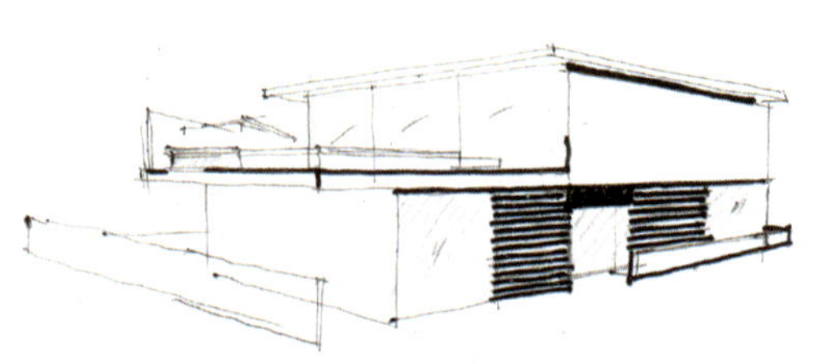 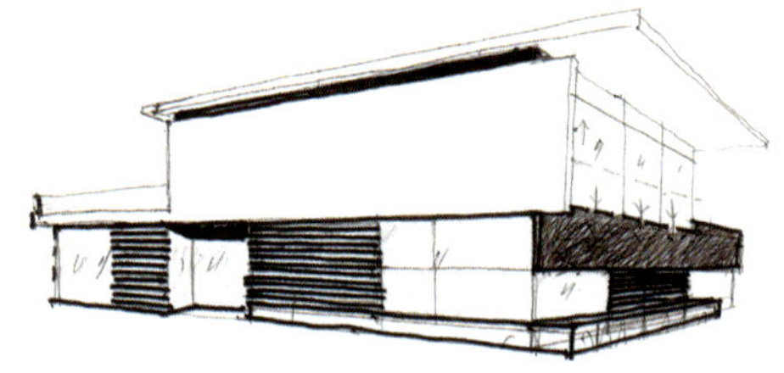 

Claudio Nardi architetto - tutti i diritti riservati

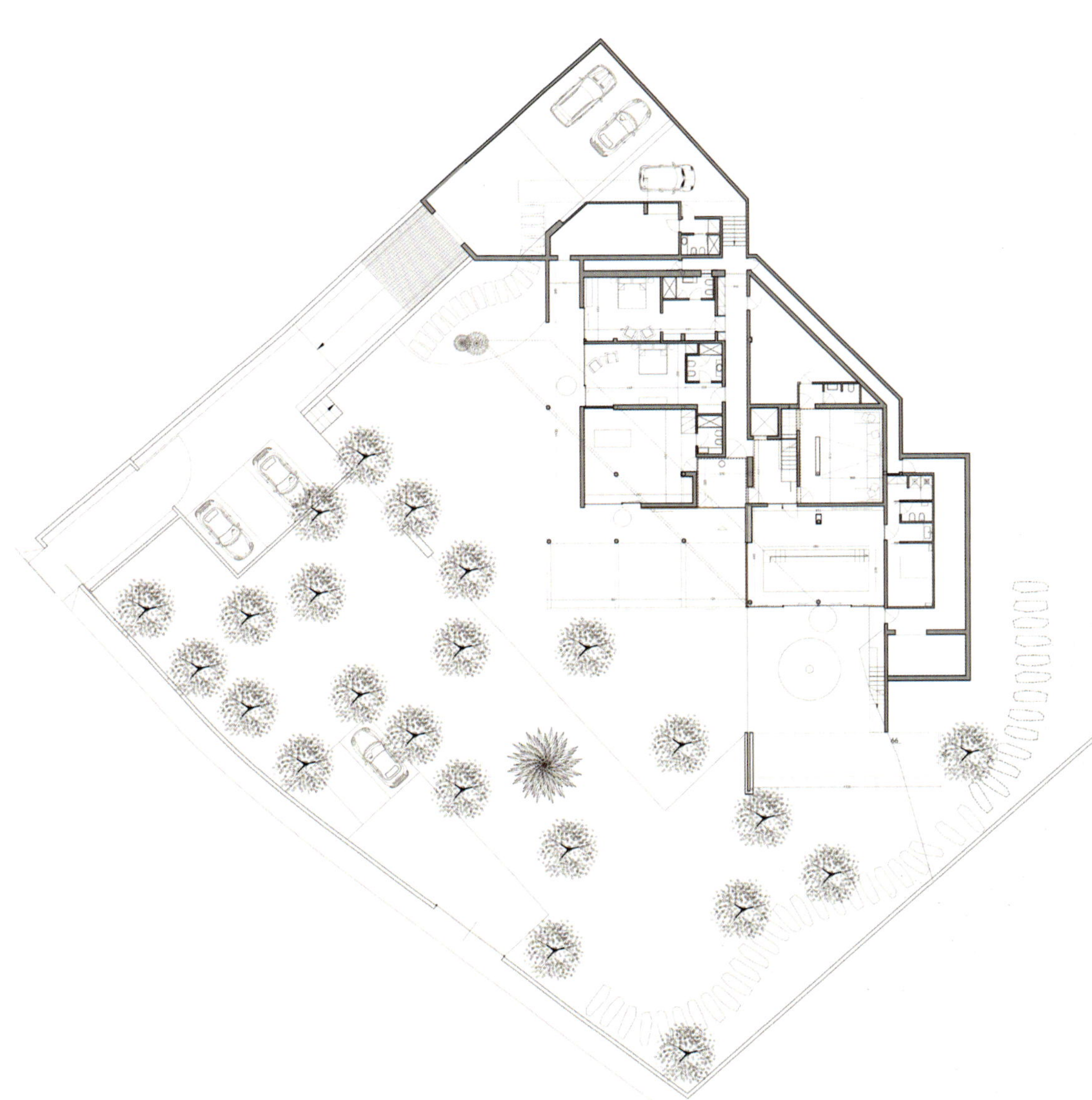

Villa Versilia, Tuscany, Italy, 2017

A pavillion in a park, integrating nature with form.

The villa is inspired by Meditteranean rationalist architecture and the organic materials of Tuscany. Stone, stucco, wood, natural light, trees and vegetation are not only interconnected with the building, but intersect it becoming the material and form.

A game of shadow boxes, the primary volume made of horizontal and essential lines stretches out towards the large surrounding park, at the same time creating a new volume marked by large openings, loggias through which one sees the internal nucleus.

These large openings and the windows are framed by climbing greenery which in turn becomes the protagonist, framed by the architectural form.

Residential Complex Dong Shan Condo, Beijing, China, 2017

Dynamic prestige floating in space and light.

A combination of design and decor in a signature modern key. The dynamic plays of light and volumes distinguish the apartments, open spaces that flow from one room to another, open yet private, elegant but not ostentatious. The use of precious materials such as Carrara marble and fine wood, the elegant, exclusively Italian furnishings and fixtures all combine to provide unique environments of contemporary luxury. The strong but warm minimalism, light and floating, as if daylight was filtering down from above, becomes comfortable and protective, light and shadow creating new volumes and depths accentuated by the varying ceiling heights and wall treatments.

ARCHITECTURE

Redesign of Piazza Matteotti, Competition, First Prize, Tavarnelle Val di Pesa, Italy, 2002

Piazza dei Ciompi, Florence, Italy, 2010

BP Studio Factory, Florence, Italy, 1999

The project connects a functional re-organization of the existing pavilions with the addition of new volumes and new surfaces, over all a new shell(a ventilated and technological skin) that creates an original relation between structure, form and image in the renovated layout. The factory had to meet not only functional requirements, it had to become also a means to communicate the reality of one business by putting in display its process of production, its image. Located at the edge of the highway, the new factory remain suspended between a cinematic perception of its image, closed within the lines stressed by the vibration of the cotto shell, and its spatial contiguity to the heterogeneous industrial landscape.

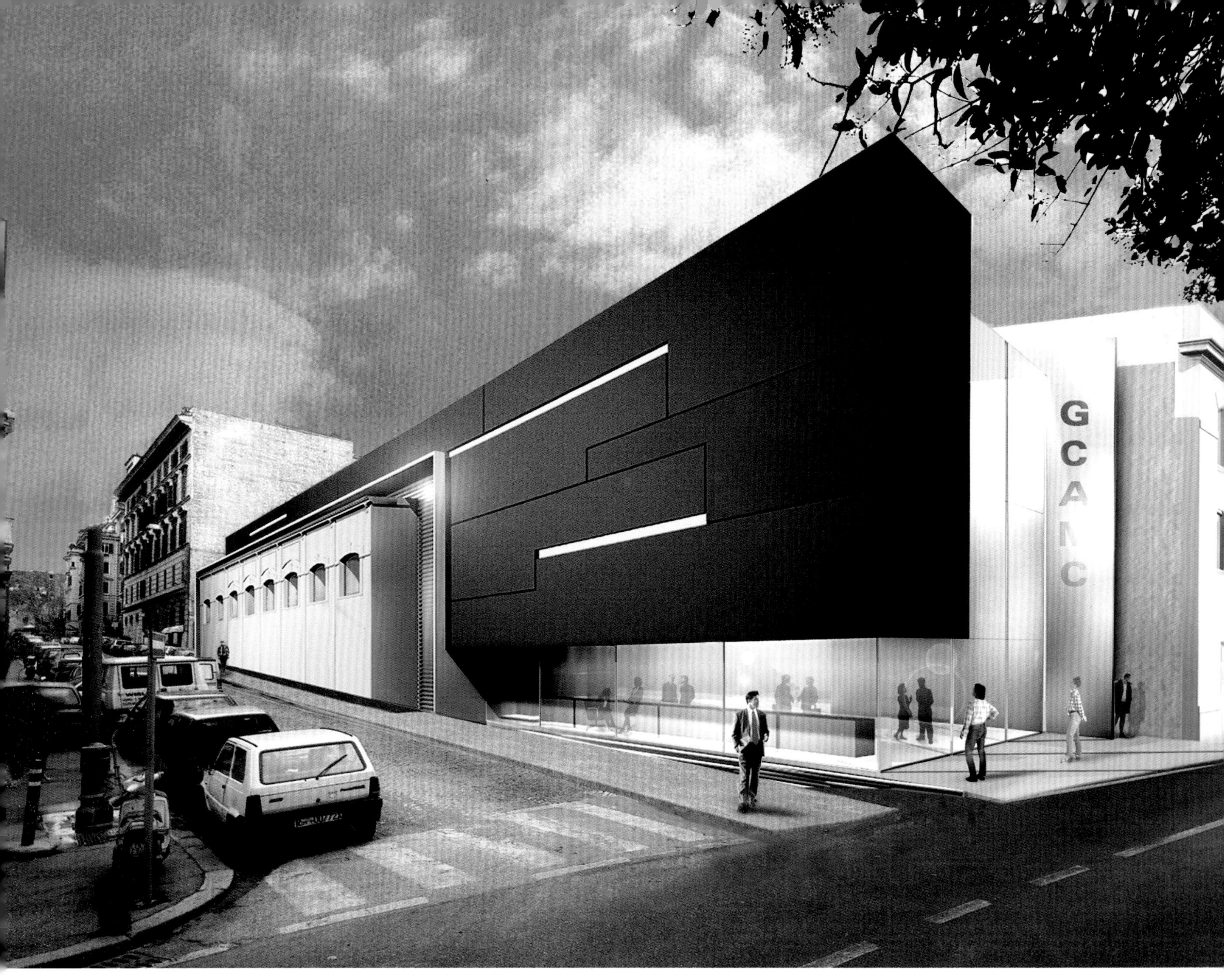

Museum of Contemporary Art, Competition, Former Peroni Area, Rome, Italy, 2000

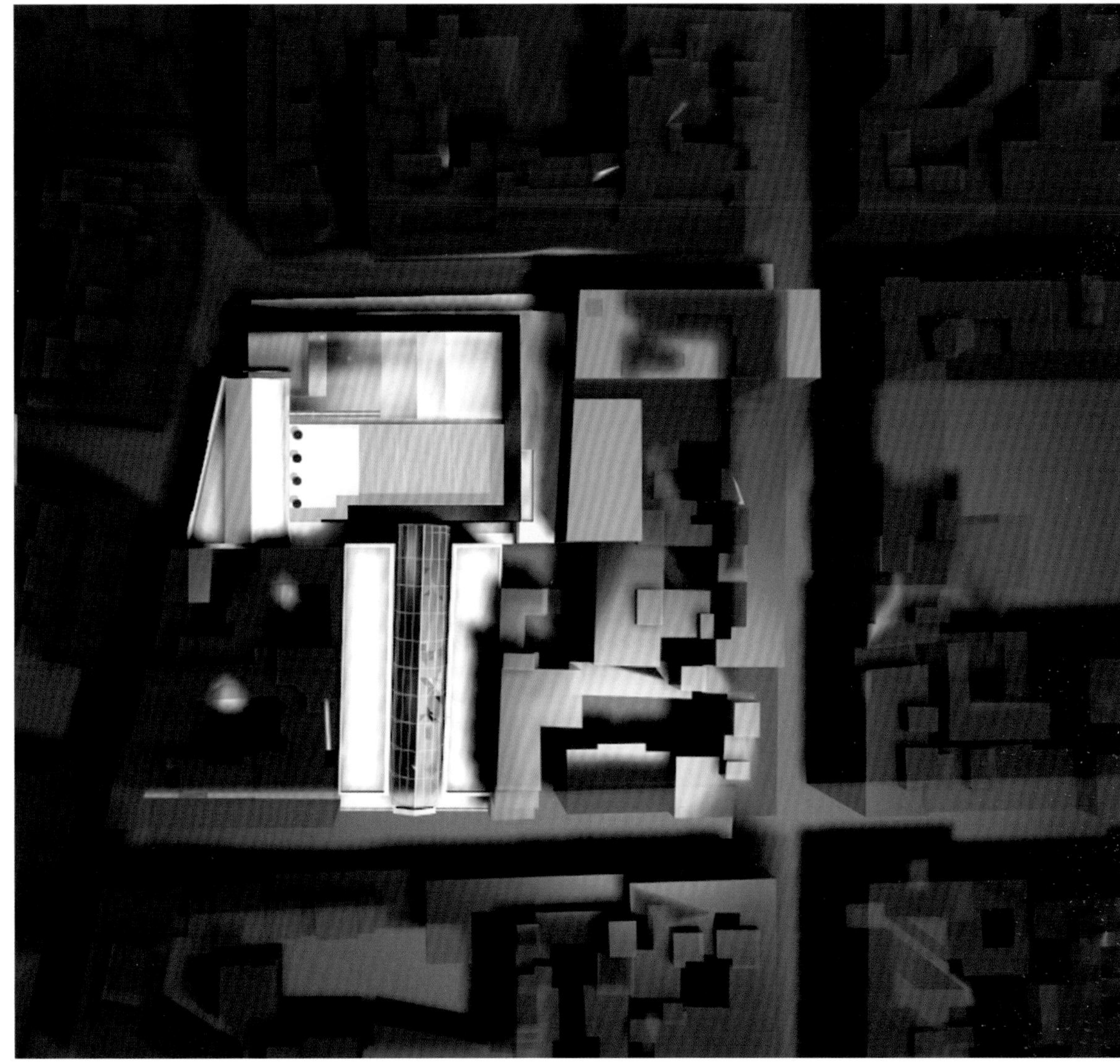

Consiag New Headquarters, Competition by Invitation, First Prize, Second Stage, Prato, Italy, 2000

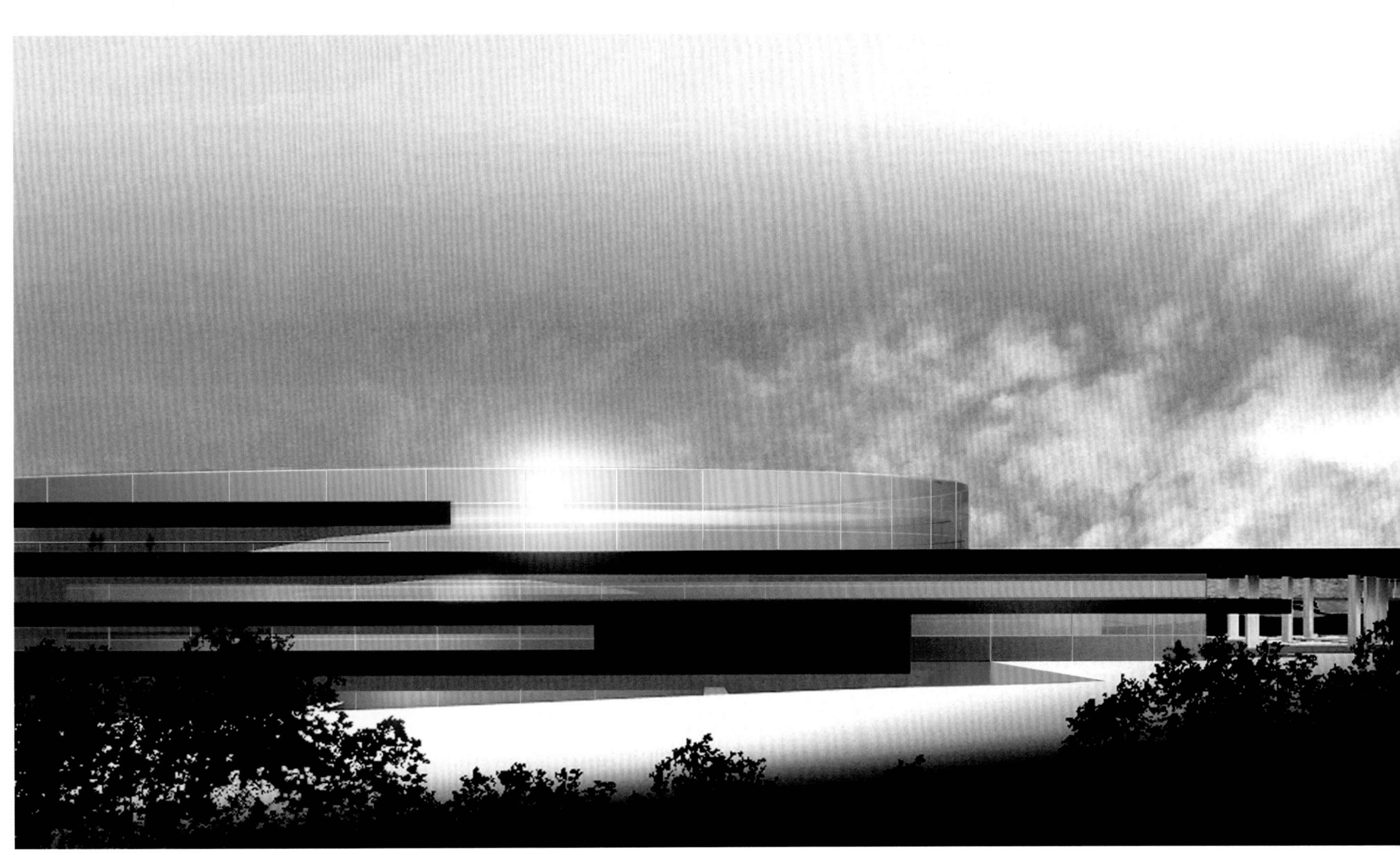

Costantini Museum, Competition, Buenos Aires, Argentina, 1998

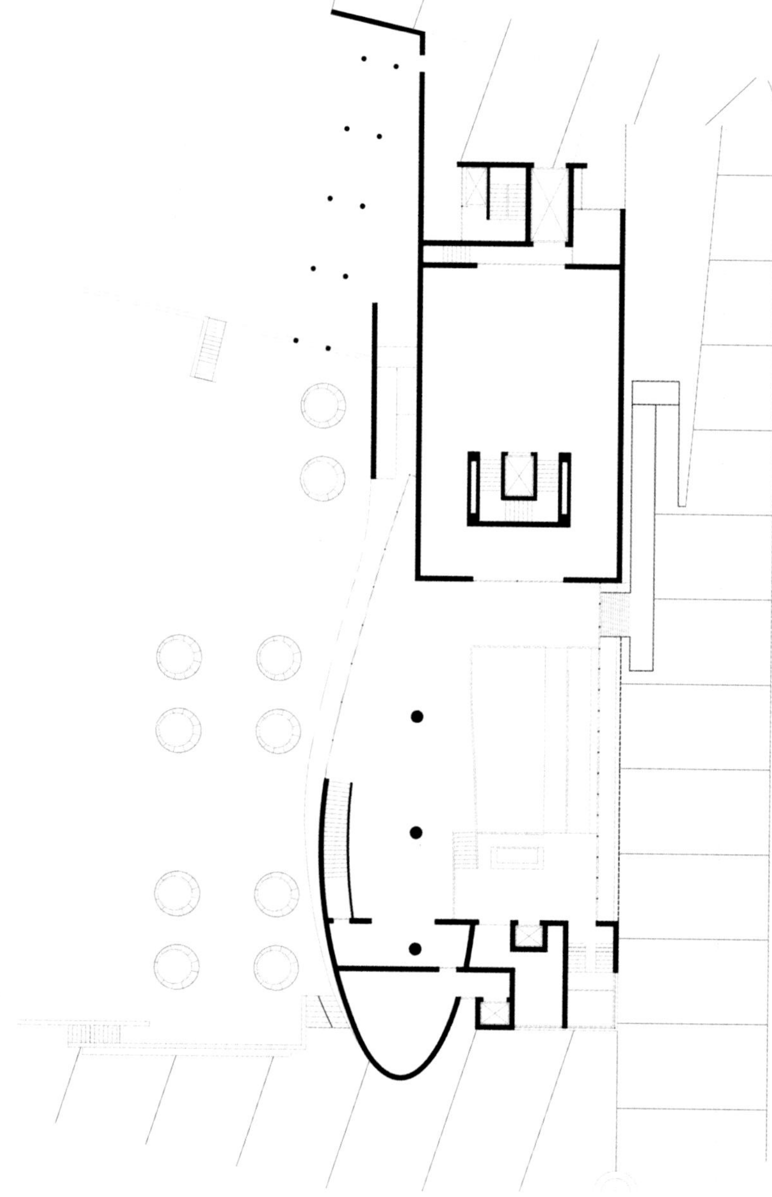

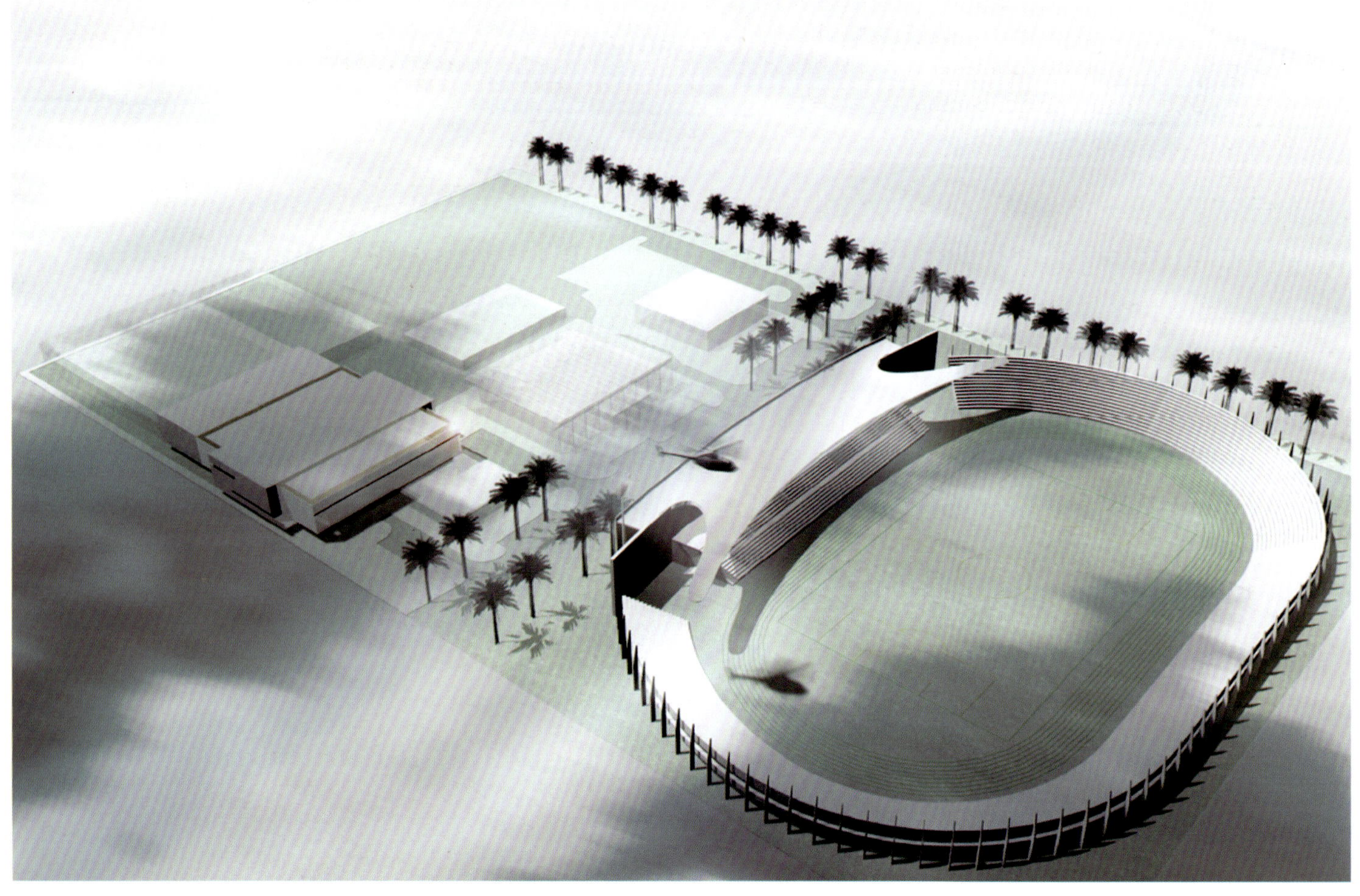

Grandstand Al Jazeera Sporting Club, Competition by Invitation, Abu Dhabi, E.A.U., 2001

A structure in flight, hovering like an eagle.

The composition mainly plays on the horizontal-vertical relations between the grandstand and its roofing, exploiting the notable contrast between the enormity of the stand – made of decorative concrete – and the structural simplicity of the cantilever roof. The shape of the roof is designed for the double function of offering repair and shade to the stand and, at the same time, allowing the light to come inside and illuminate the field. The shape of the roofing "wings" emphasises the volume's lightness and gives it a sense of movement.

The cantilevered roof is anchored to a slightly curved building behind the grandstand and is "protected" by a curved wall, larger than the building which embraces the grandstand. The building contains a dense network of paths, corridors, intersecting aisles and lifts that can comfortably handle the flows of the crowds together with utilities for the spectators, the players, the VIPs. A lightweight glass and steel box, suspended from the roof, hosts the VVIP seats.

Peterhof Golf Club, St. Petersburg, Russia, 2018

Waterfront, Competition, Lignano Sabbiadoro, Italy, 2001

The tradition of the grand beach terrace in a modern key.

Born from the idea that the "waterfront" is not simply the meeting point of the city with the sea but has all the potential to become the site of a new urban centrality. The leading issues covered in the project: the promenade architecture and the relationship between city centre and sea introducing a system of new functions: the creation of a panoramic commercial axis, the reconstruction of a natural environment, the development of a linked monorail system, the introduction of highly qualified functions and new settlements.

The new pedestrian promenade, positioned to the sea at a higher altitude than the road, contributes to the new identity of the landscape and its enjoyment as well as to open the city more to the sea. A long pier departs from the promenade and becomes the connection with the new "seafront terrace" located 500 metres from the shoreline, a building with nightly entertainment and an outdoor space with furnished roof terrace and pool in the centre. Through the glass walls that immerse themselves in the water of the sea, it is possible to observe the seabed throughout the year.

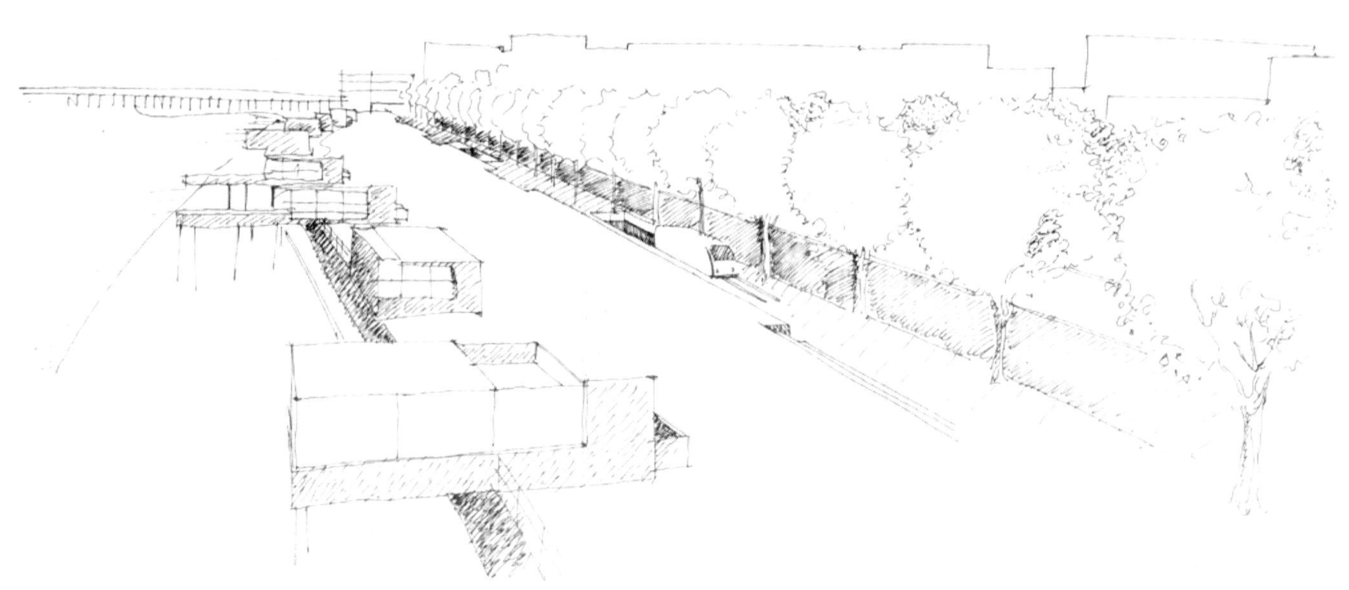

Multiplex Cinema, Campi Bisenzio, Florence, Italy, 2001

The four facades are designed differently taking into account the needs they must respond to, the perception of which is achieved through the play of volumes and materials. The entire structure is marked by a marked horizontality emphasized by the use of natural, traditional materials, capable of aging well, such as cotto, here reinterpreted in a contemporary way, as color and texture.

WHO Headquarters Building Extension, Competition, Geneva, Switzerland, 2014

The vibrating surface of the whitewashed brise-soleil cladding is inspired by the regular and modern appearance of the façade of the adjacent building, an abstract surface from which, in different positions, we see the emergence of volumes, covered with slabs of the same white marble, extruded at different depths and projected towards the garden inside the complex.
The building rests on an equipped plate, consisting of levels -1 and -2, covered with terraces and hanging gardens that visually give way to the garden.

Music School, Competition, Posen, Poland, 2014

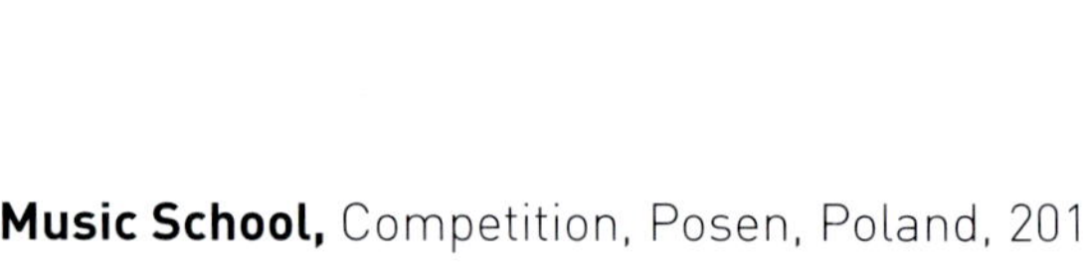

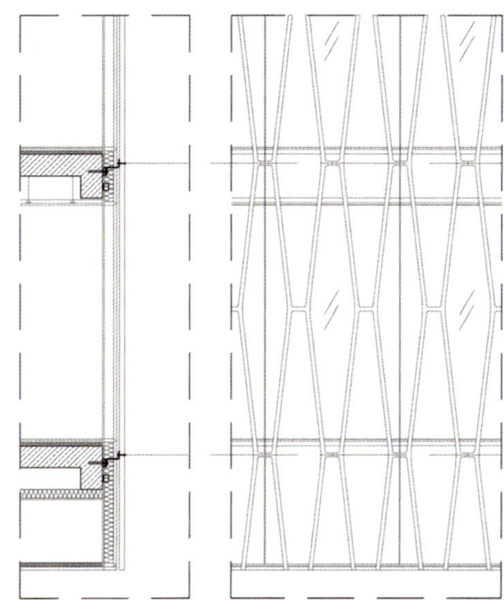

Alarico Resort Hotel and Wellness Centre, Carolei, Cosenza, Italy, 2004

The hotel overlooks the deep gravina created by the river Busento. The rooms are partially underground, following the contour lines, almost all facing the valley and covered with hanging gardens and terraces. The common areas are instead organized inside a large glazed volume, partially suspended, with a vertiginous gradient, on the river bed, passing from the discreet, hypogeal construction, to the reflections of a contemporary, elegant, light and decisive sign.

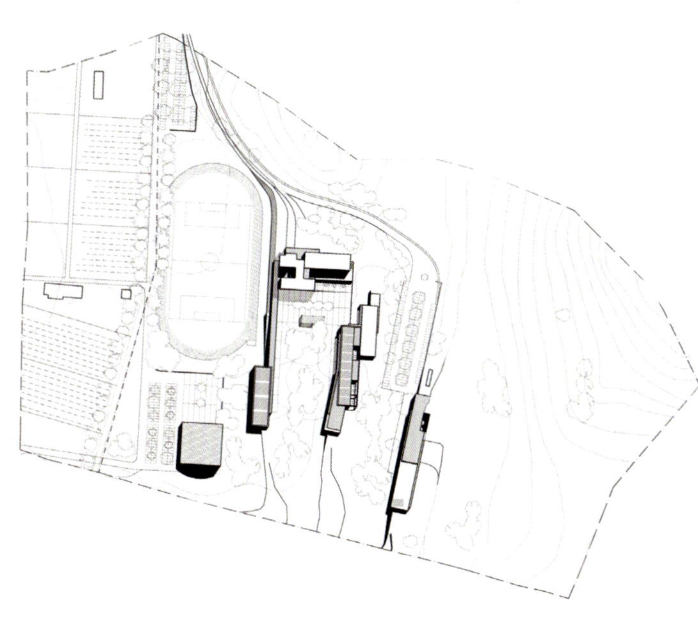

Redevelopment and Extension of the Professional Institute for Hotel Services,
Competition, Second Prize, Tortoli, Italy 2004

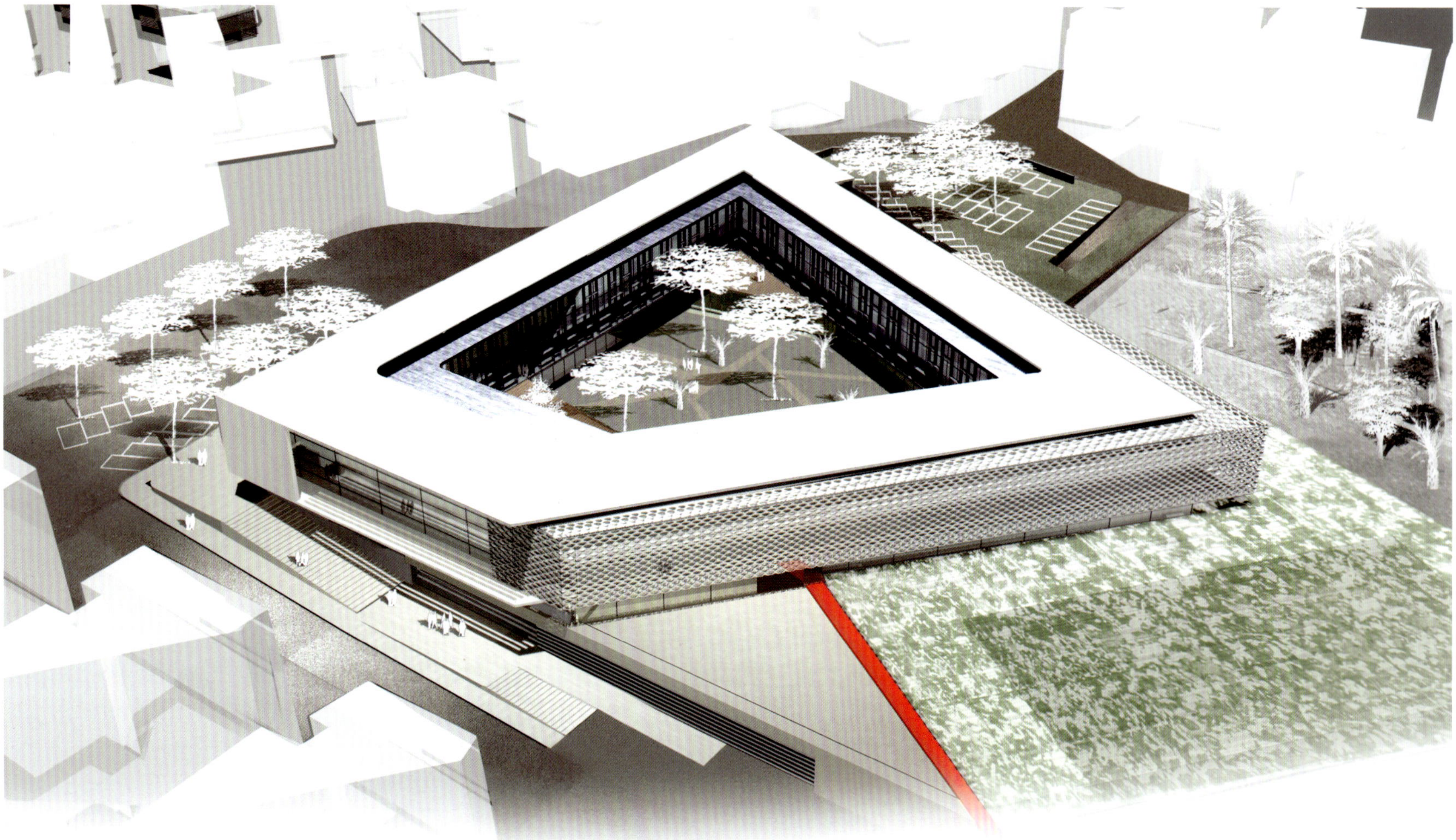

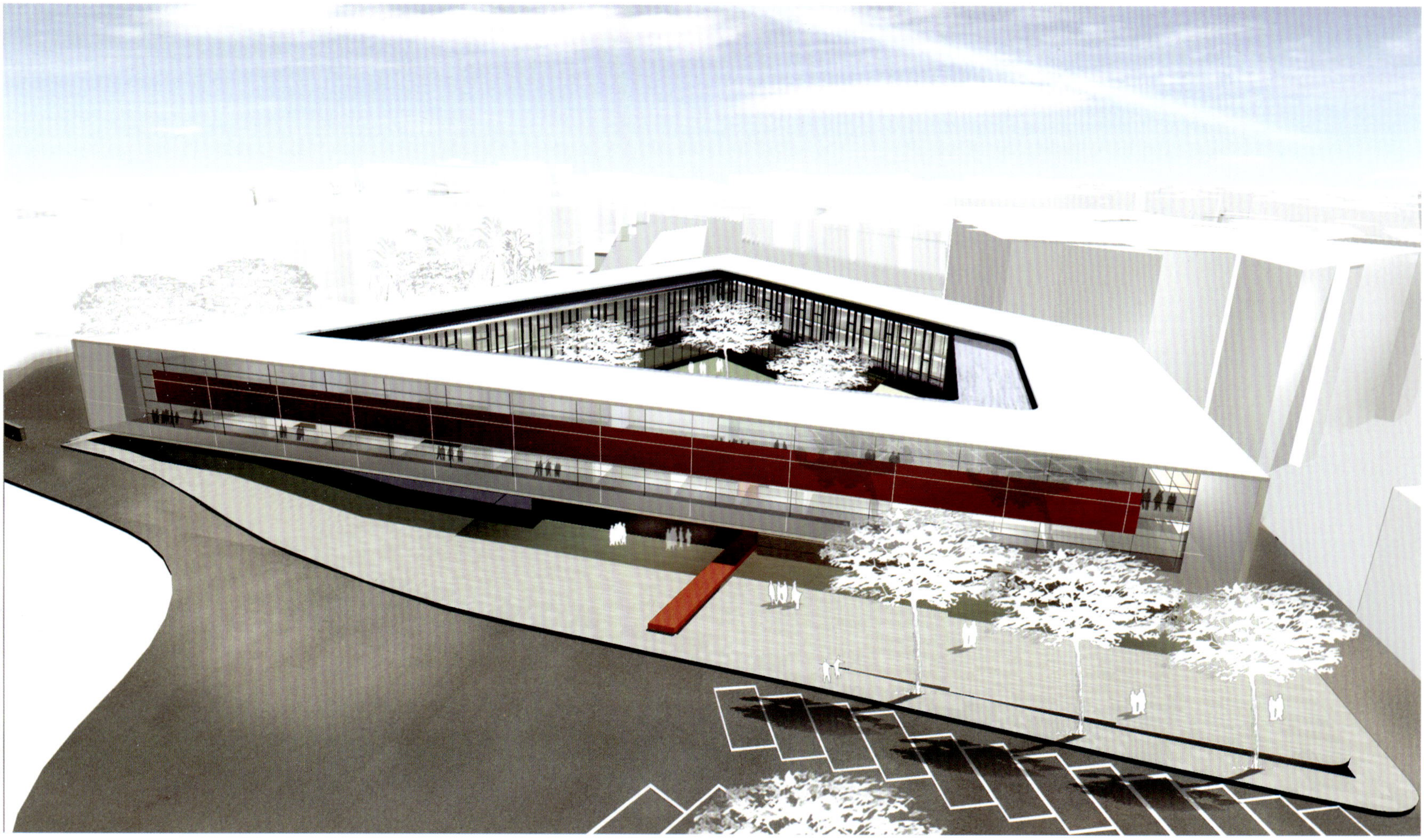

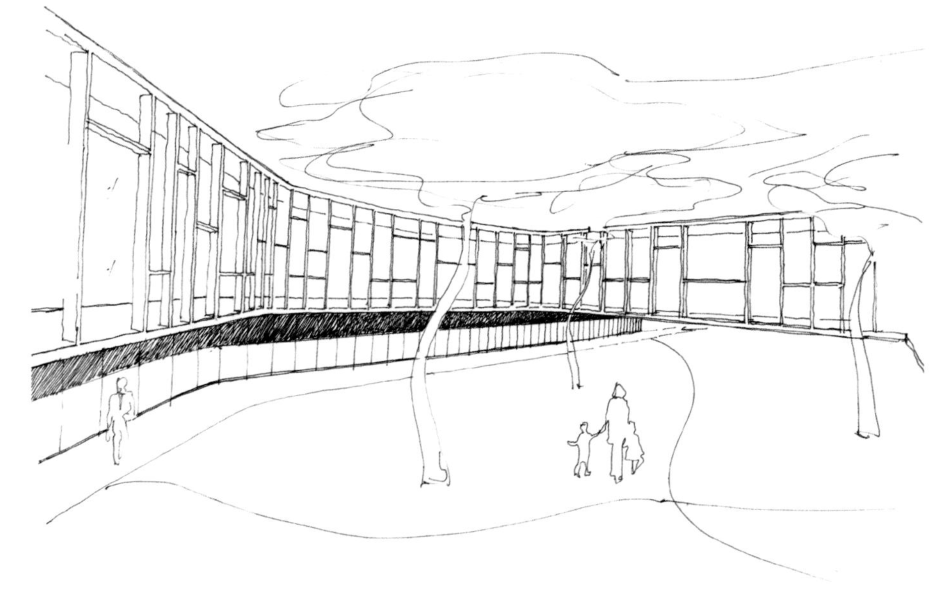

Calabria Region Offices, Competition, Reggio Calabria, Italy, 2005

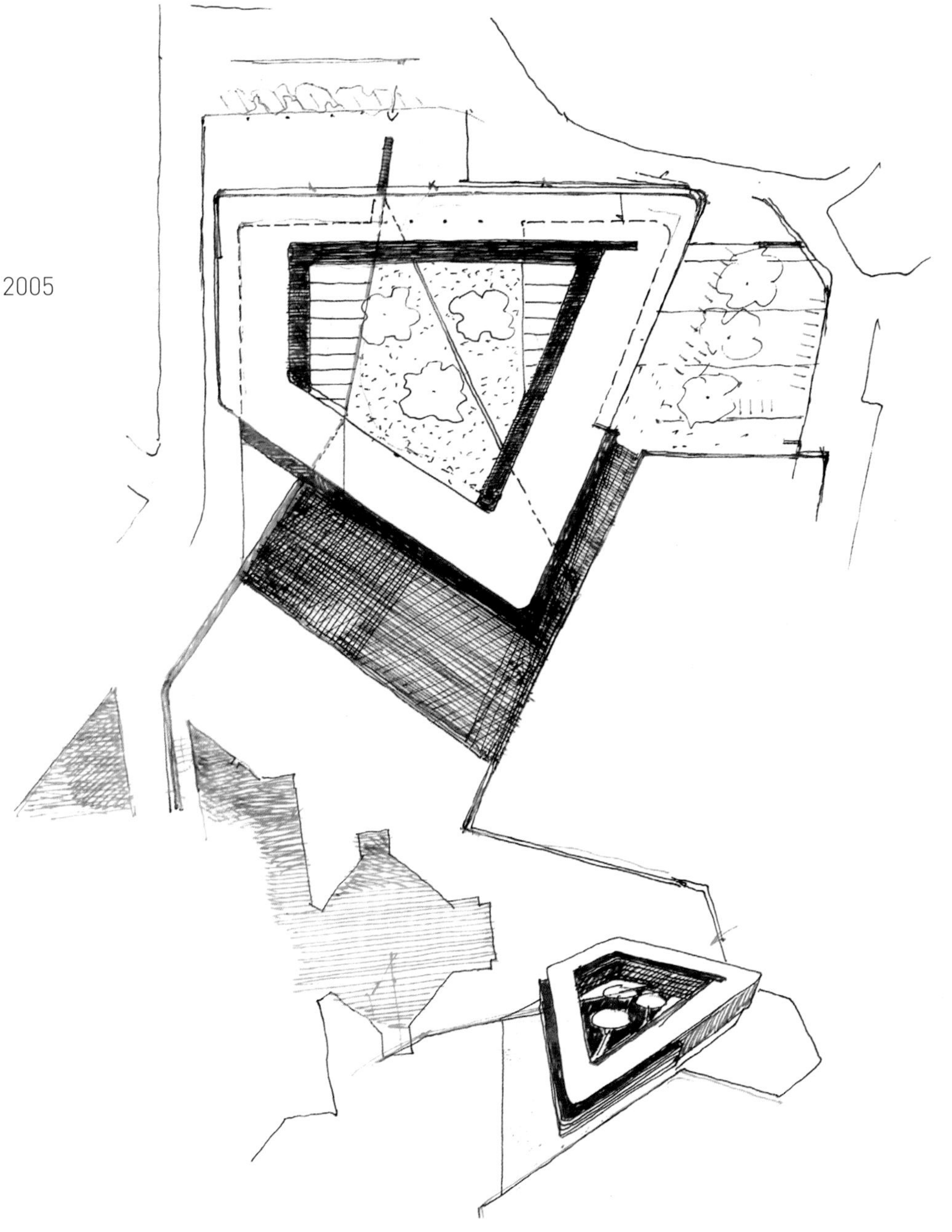

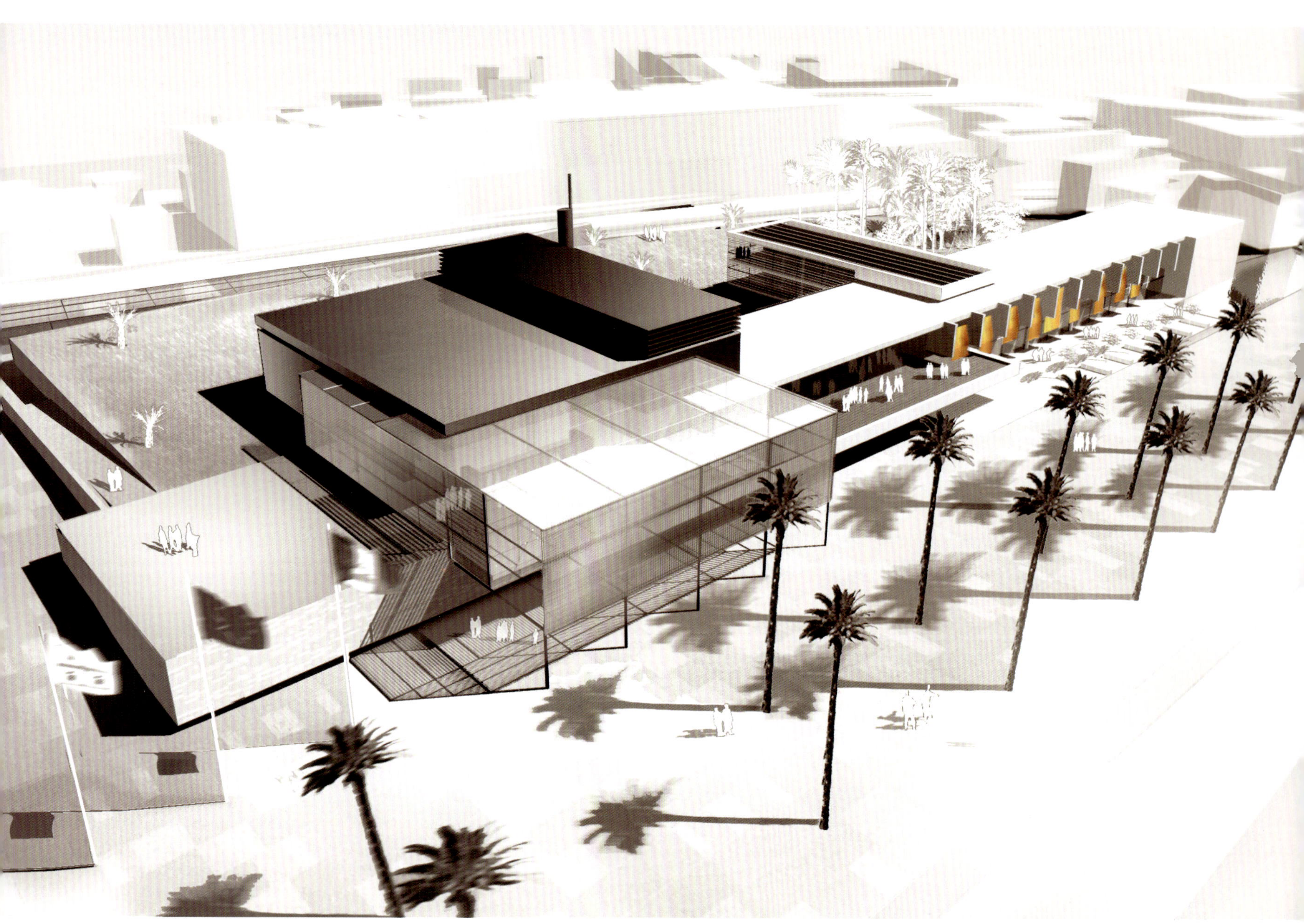

Redevelopment of the "Ex Saica" Area, Competition, Third Prize, Alghero, Italy, 2005

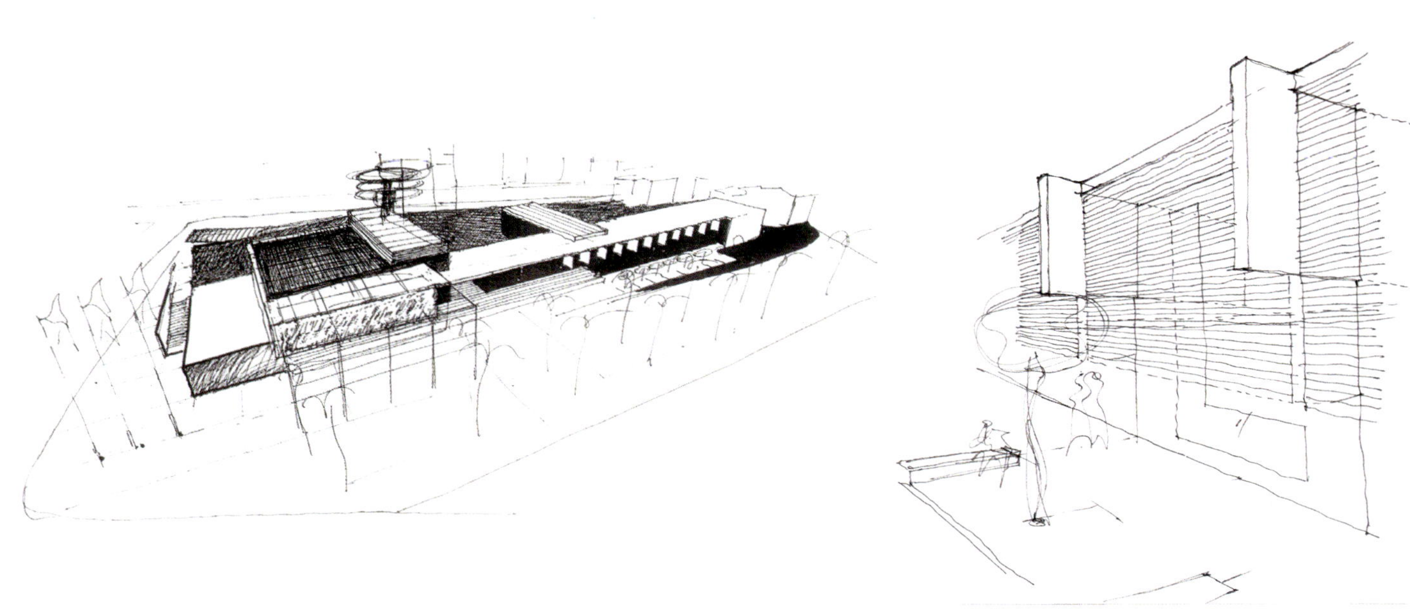

Chamber of Commerce, Competition, Honorable Mention, Prato, Italy, 2006

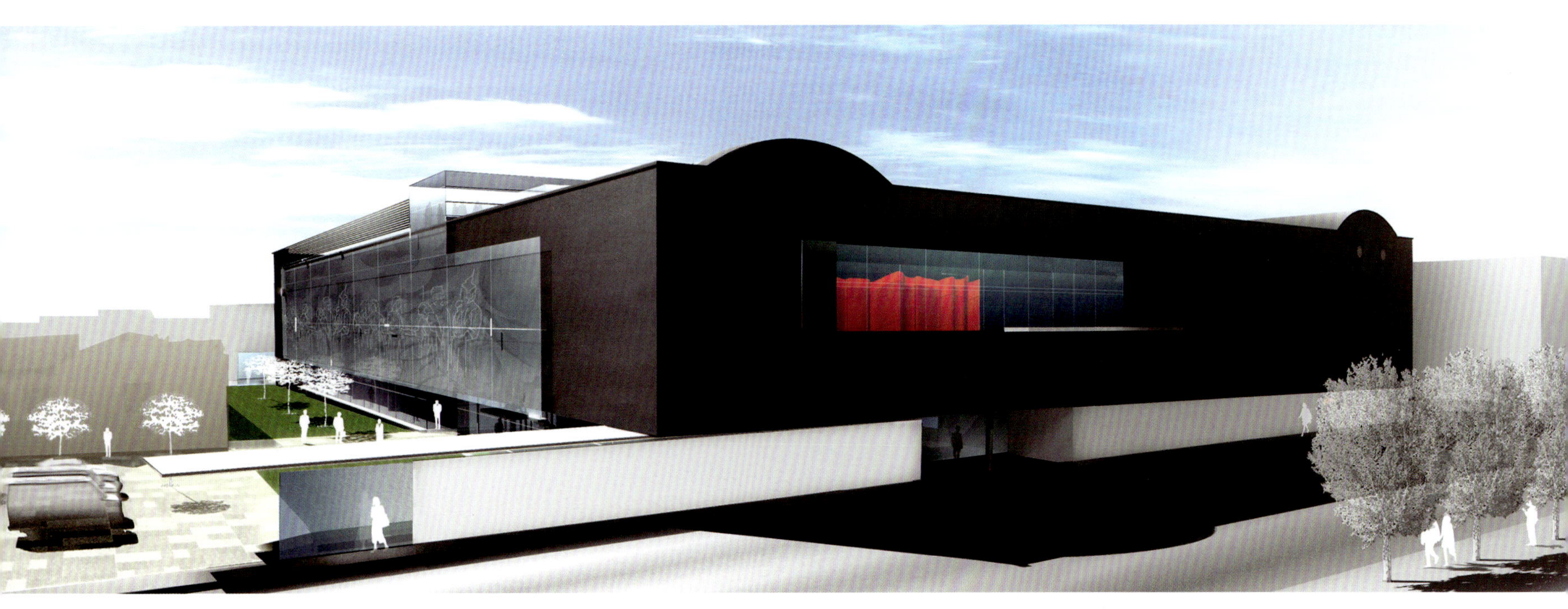

223

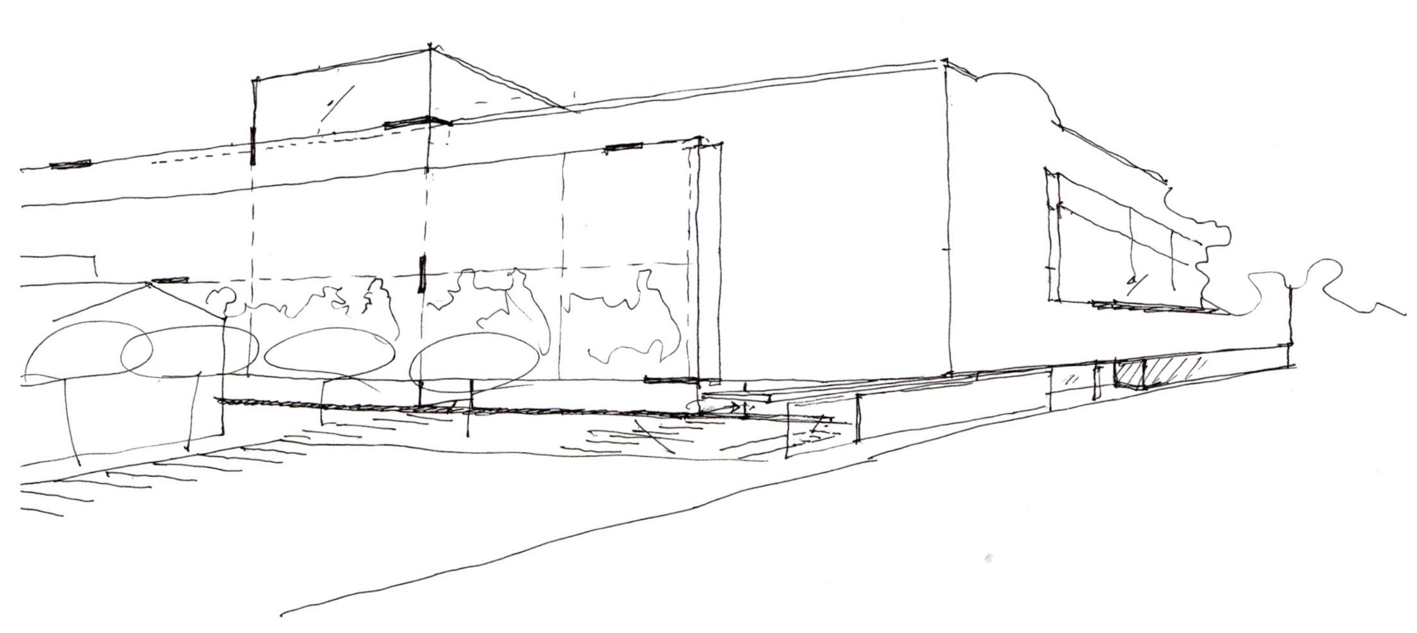

Absolute Design Ideas Competition,
Honorary Mention, Mississauga, Canada, 2006

Vertex Tower, Project, Amman, Jordan, 2006

Vertex Tower forms part of the most ambitious urban redevelopment project at the edge of the historic city centre of Amman. Originally the area which covers some 30 hectares in the Abdali quarter, had been designated for military use. Now it is a mixture of residential and commercial spaces, parking facilities, cinemas, library and gymnasium are all gathered in a wide complex of buildings defined by four towers, each over 110 metres high and lower complementary structures. Of these, the tower and related buildings are characterised by sharp floating planes in light grey stone which hover almost detached from the building, intersecting each other and the other panels sheathed in dark blue electroplated aluminium.

Extensive glass surfaces complete the tower, imparting a strong geometric sense, using irregular and asymmetrical shapes to create the vibrant and dynamic design. The solid surfaces, clad in stone or aluminium, are scored by a variable rhythm of openings and frames that punctuate the solid mass of the façades. Traditional and contemporary materials, ethereal glass and also massive material surfaces highlight the volumes into which the openings appear set as precious stones.

New Urban Center, Competition, First Prize, Veliko Tarnovo, Bulgaria, 2018

Port Authority Headquarters, Competition, First Prize, Marina di Carrara, Italy, 2007

The perception of the sea, its proximity, but perhaps even the palm trees lined up along the border of Colombo Avenue, more than other references, provide the creative path of this building with its horizontal lines. Proportions and materials refer to the language of Mediterranean architecture and Italian rationalism, austere, massive and transparent, bright and sensitive to the natural play of lights and shadows.

A solid building in its structural features and exterior sandstone finishes but made "light" by glass ventilated façades and sun shades in stainless steel mesh. Along Colombo Avenue, the elevation facing onto the avenue is accompanied by a deep, welcoming, wood-clad portico, as if part of the interior façades, a technologically variant of teak which diffuses its eternal references to the language of the sea.

Above the portico a large terrace opens out, protected by an equally deep porch that reaches towards the avenue without creating a barrier but only transparency in the relationship with the city. The portico is like a theatrical set that frames the sky above the sea from one side and the white marble Mountains on the other.

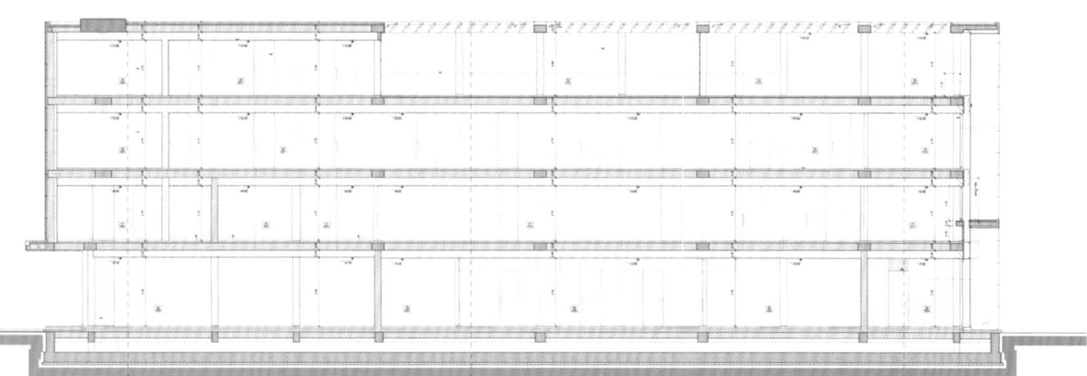

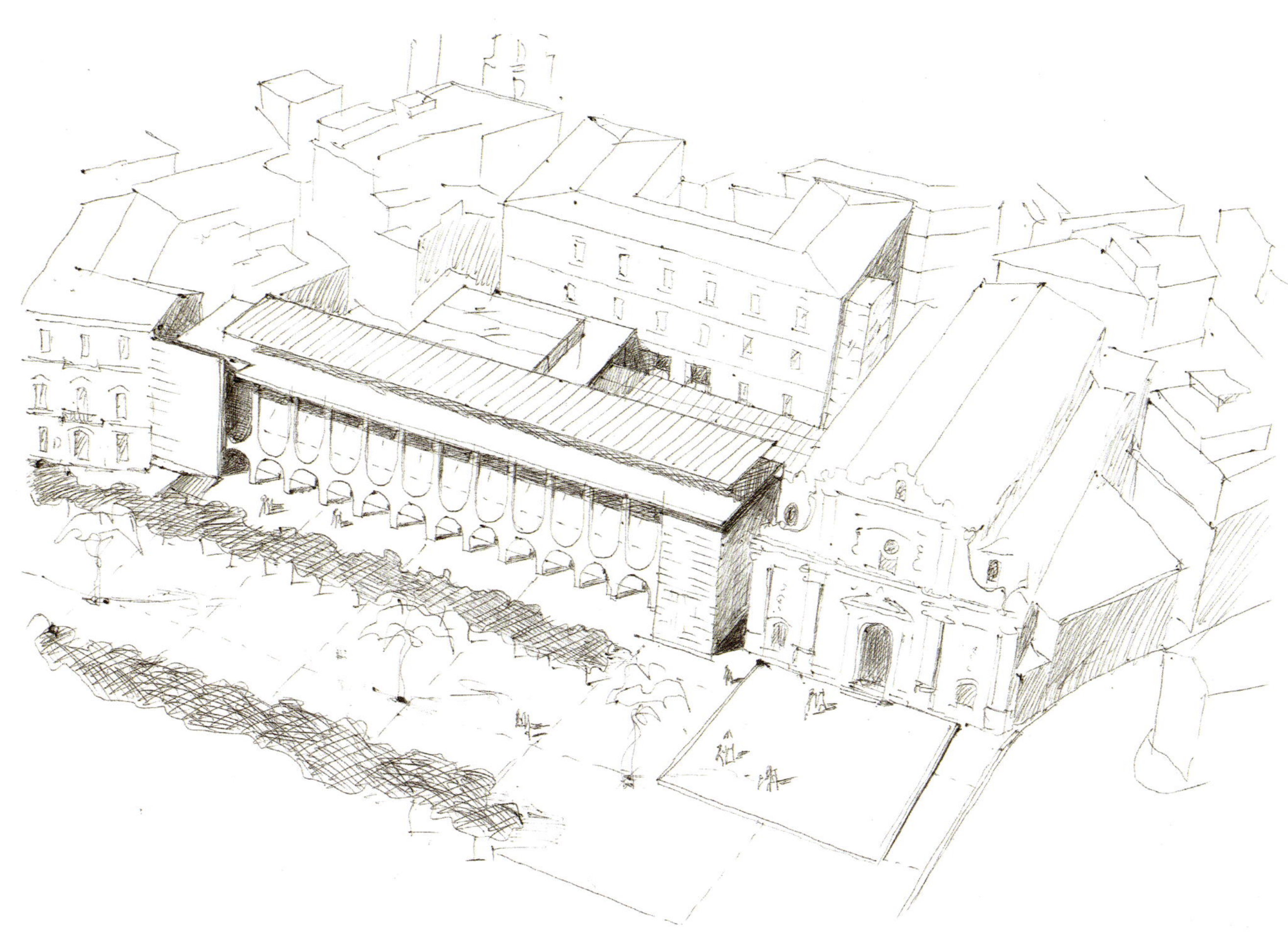

Expansion and Refurbishment of Educational Facility, Competition, Second Prize, Scicli, Ragusa, Italy, 2009

Commerce One, Amman, Jordan, 2007

Creating the individual amongst the anonymous.

The idea of this office building was to distance it from the proliferation of meaningless glass boxes, characteristic of modern business centres the world over.

A contrast to the symmetrical, ordered traditional arrangement of volumes.

The concept springs from a theatrical interpretation of space and surface.

A solid white band frames the large glass wall screened with wire mesh and this luminous volume is imbedded into the solid grey stone mass of the building.

Museum of Contemporary Art, Competition, First Prize, Krakow, Poland, 2010

Revitalisation, creating between memory and future.

MOCAK, the new Museum of Contemporary Art of Krakow, built on the site of the historic Oscar Schindler Factory, is a project poised between memory and future, opening a new major chapter in the cultural life of the city.

The industrial symbolism, evoked by the typical existing saw-tooth roof of the buildings, has represented the icon that has inspired the whole project. A 10-metre high wing of crude, industrial concrete acts as manifest and junction between the main road and the meandering sequence of itineraries and exhibition pavilions that leads the visitor deep into the area. A new architecture, weightless and gleaming, the dark fibre concrete cladding and the saw-tooth roof in titanium-zinc embrace the existing buildings and the new pavilions and combine them in a unique organism.

The building is diffused, not monolithic, characterised by the harmonious sum of many requirements, such as the need for strong overall visibility and the aesthetic and functional integration of the existing structures.

In fact, a choice was made for a building that did not surpass the height of the existing buildings, going down rather than up, thus entering instead into a dialogue with those structures through the common denominator of the factory roof reference.

The new building unfolds on two levels; the ground floor (height 390 cm) and the lower level (heights between 450 and 600 cm). It is completely independent from the existing buildings for reasons of safety and static load. The disposition of the spaces is already clear from outside the complex, highlighted by the anthracite grey wall in resin-cement which gestures from the entrance plaza, drawing the visitor into the museum itself through the glass façade.

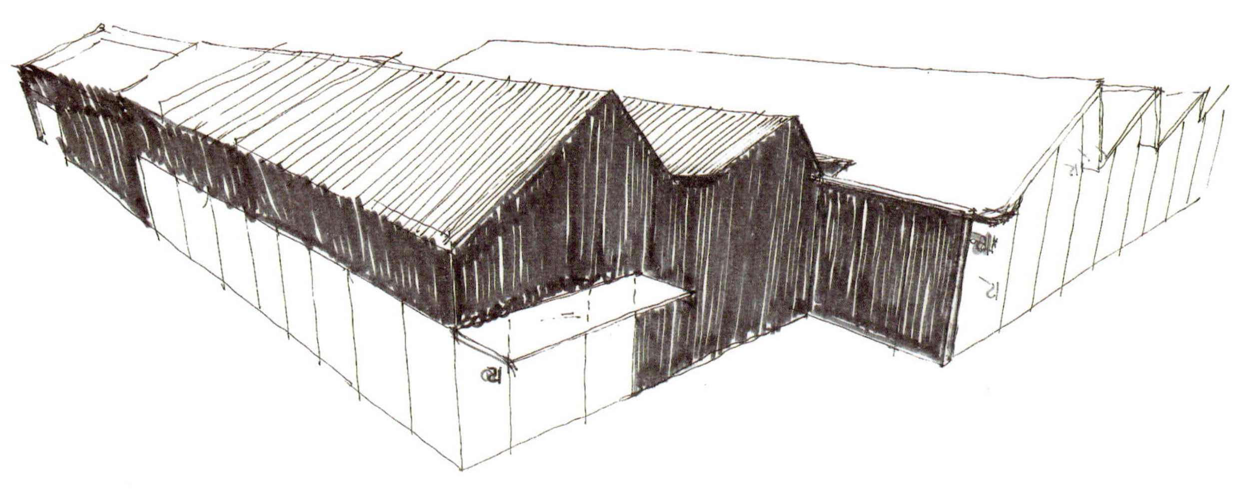

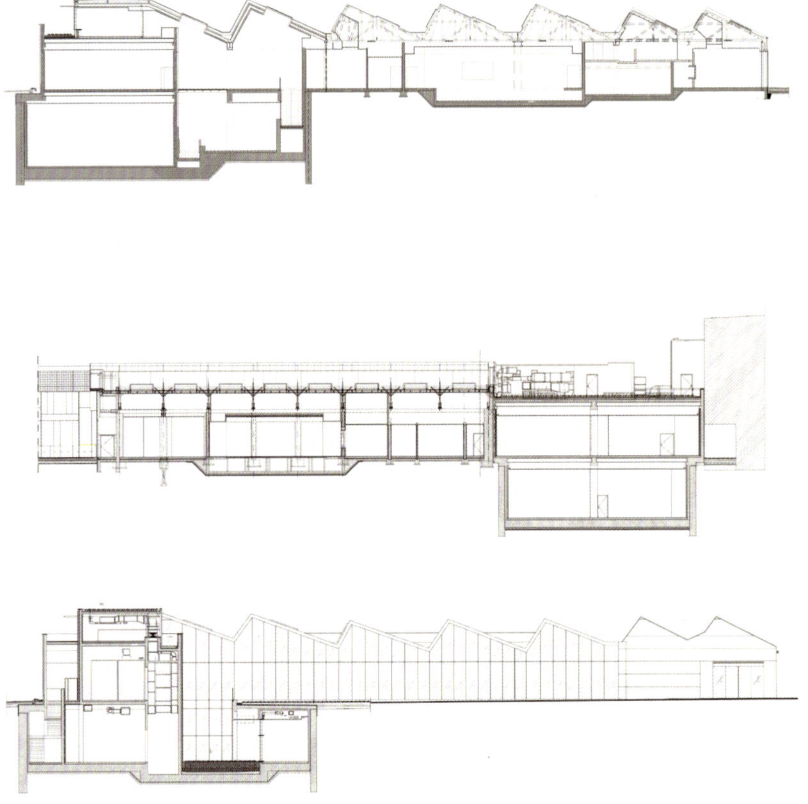

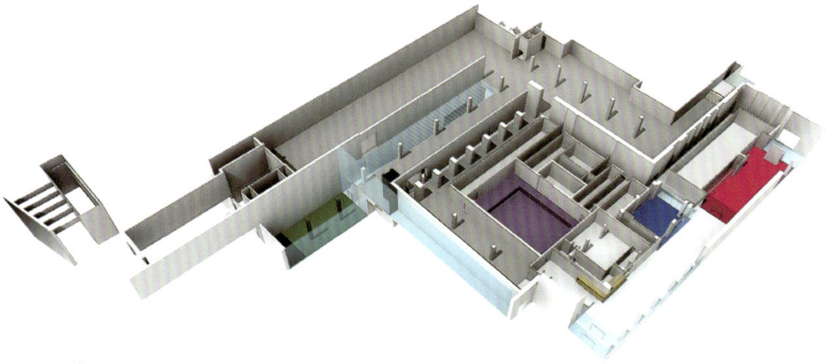

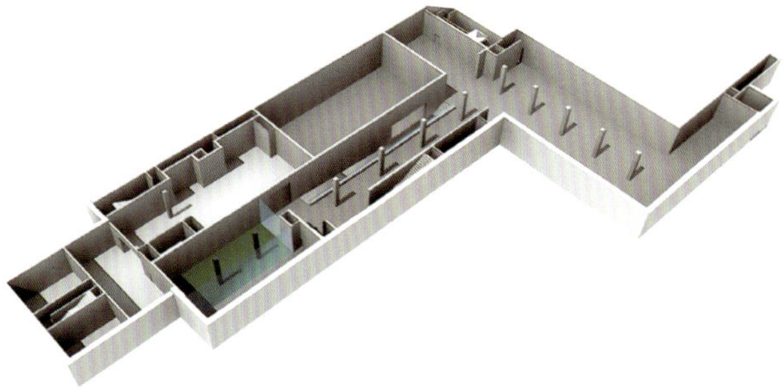

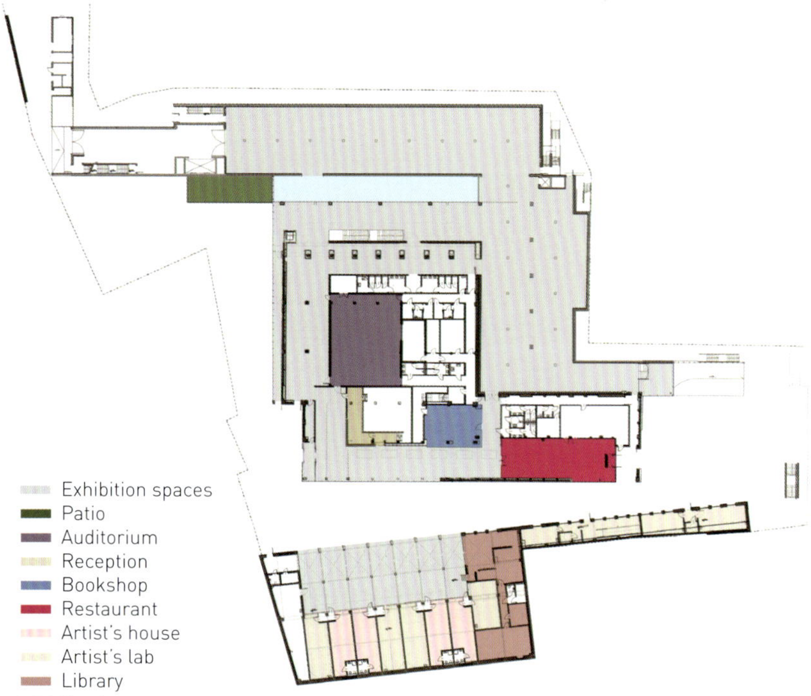

Exhibition spaces
Patio
Auditorium
Reception
Bookshop
Restaurant
Artist's house
Artist's lab
Library
Services

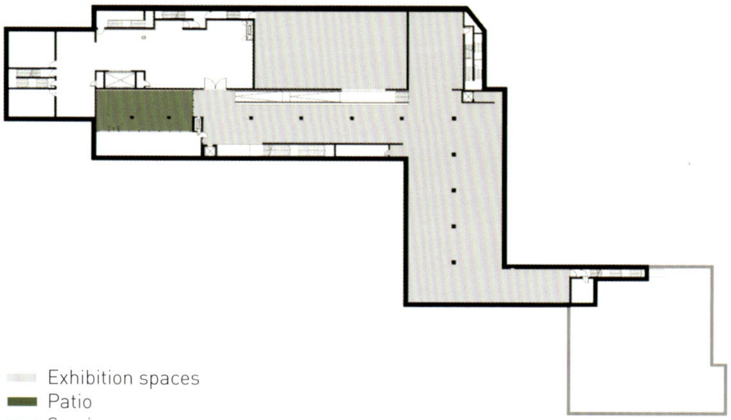

Exhibition spaces
Patio
Services

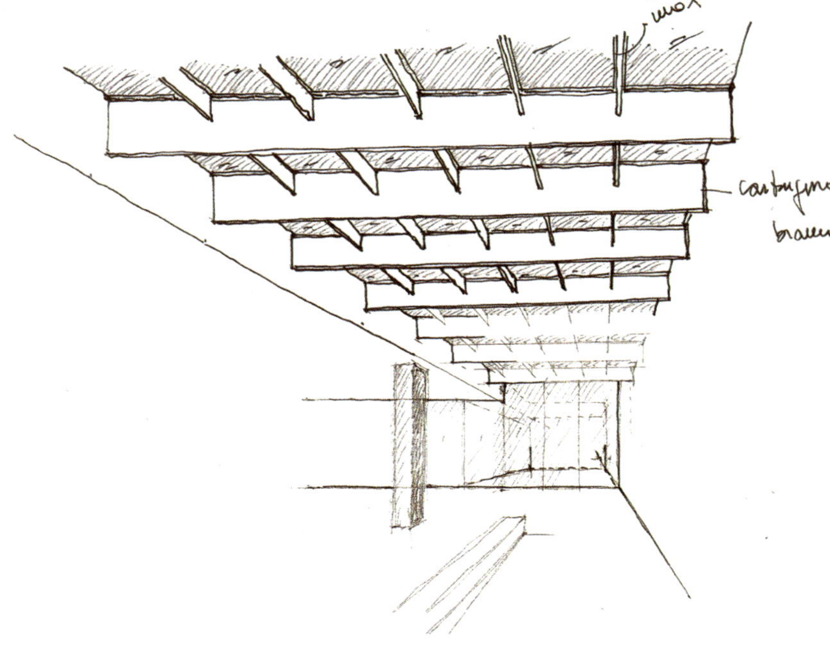
inox
carpinleno
bianco

Fabryka Oskara Schindlera - Emalia

FABRYKA O

SPRZĘT-BUD
KOWALSKI

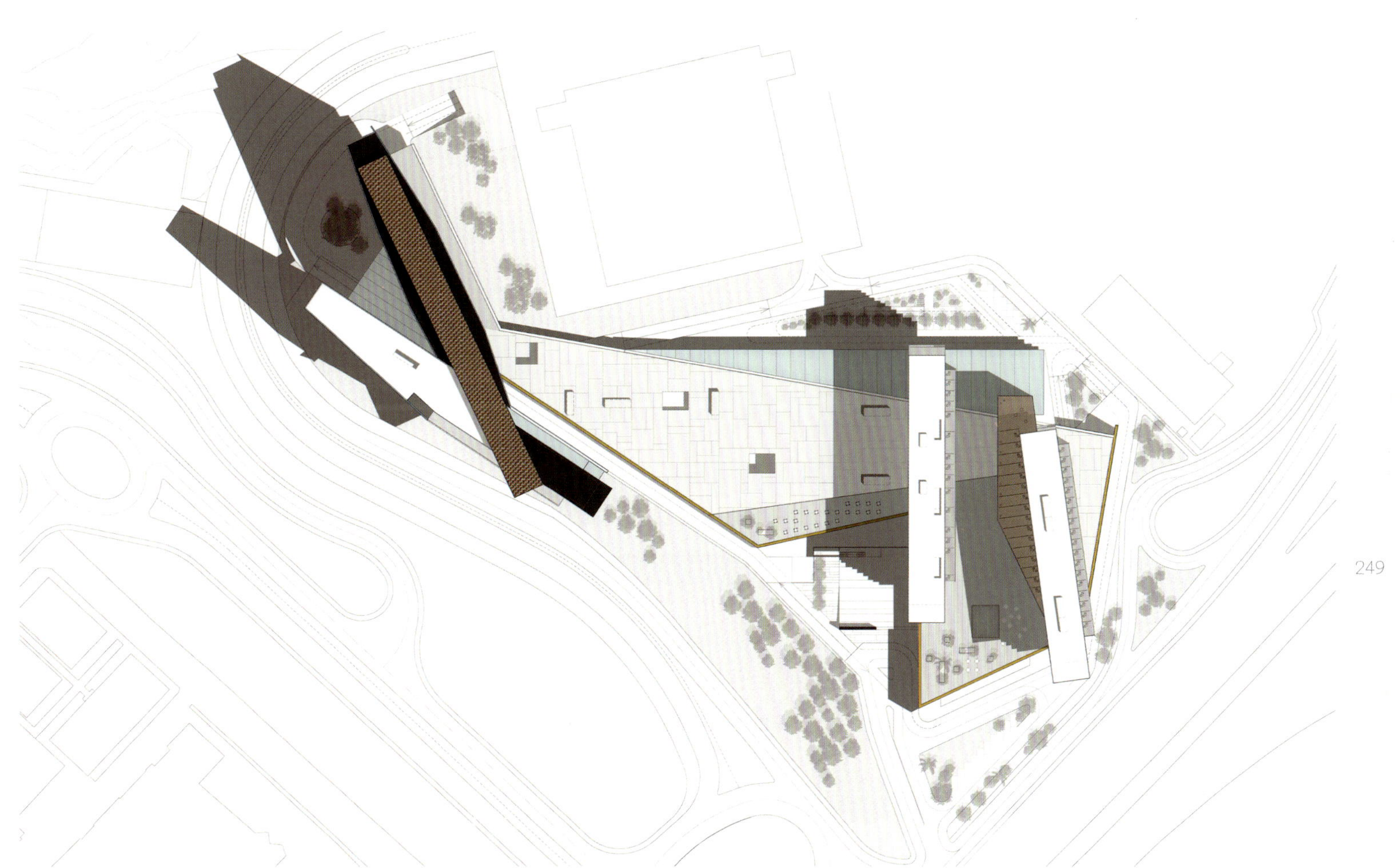

Milad Complex, Competition, Teheran, Iran, 2011

Re-design Scogli Rossi, Competition, Tortoli, Italy, 2011

Public Service Hall, Competition, Chiatura, Georgia, 2012

This is a small but evocative public space. A large tree-lined square covered by a deep and thin loggia represents the connection with the city, the two buildings that are intertwined, tell, all around, underlined by the two bright steel colors, their different functions, exactly like a teather.

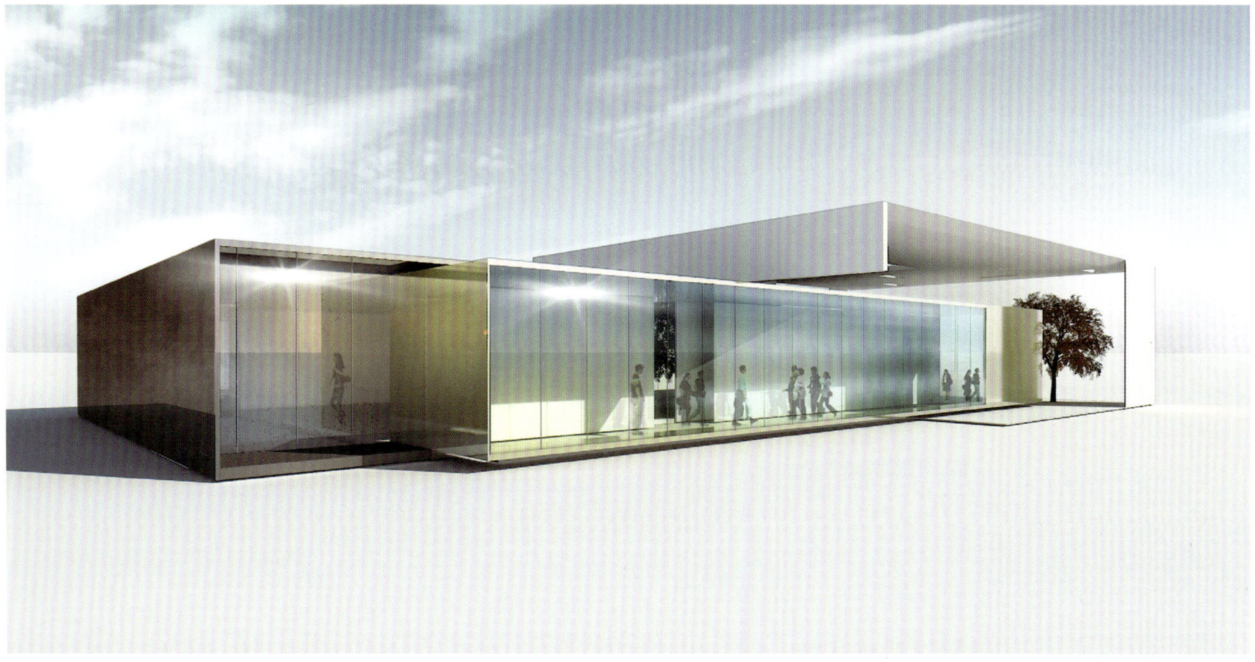

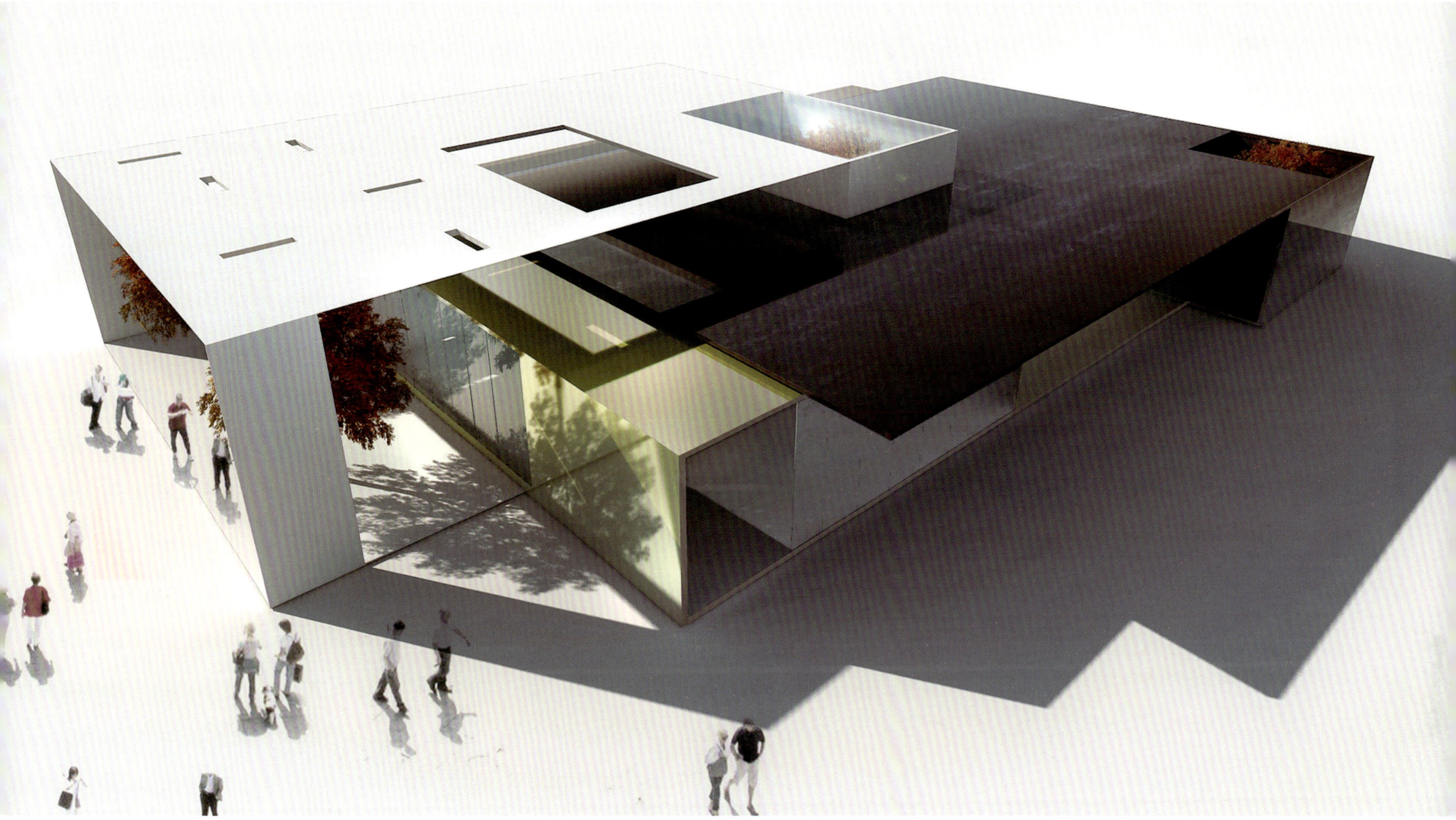

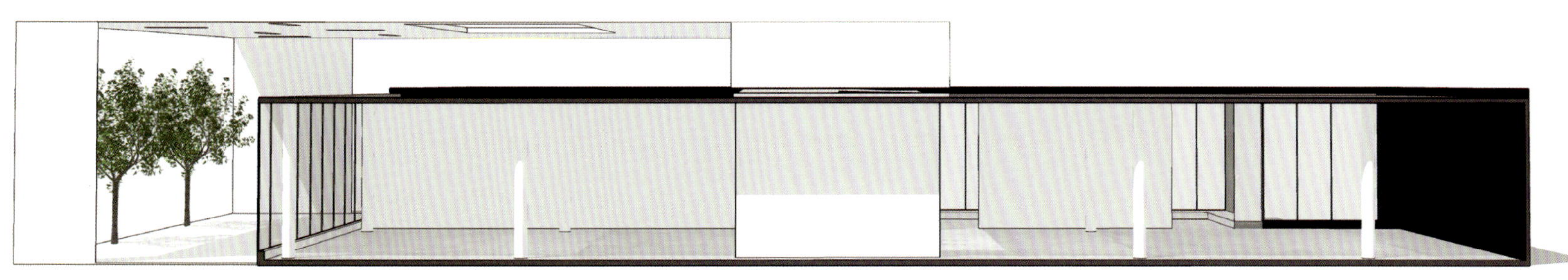

Mandragora Headquarters, Florence, Italy, 2013

Sculpting air and earth into a multi-level simultaneous existence.

The corporate headquarters of the Mandragora Fine Art Publishing House is located in an urban area close to the city centre, created to be an architecture made of light surfaces, grazing one another, almost immaterial. Over a concrete base floats a transparent and lacquered case in glass and light bronze anodised aluminium, brightness and delicacy instead of heavy, earthy solid materials.

The inspiration of the building was more the idea of transparency rather than protection, to be able to dialogue with the stones and the tired skins of the surrounding buildings.

The building, distributed on three floors, was designed on the footprint of the previous building, preserving traces and stratification, just as every urban transformation should, but then, dissatisfied with the tracks elsewhere.

The external surfaces, the new private courtyards and terraces that open inwards, the "bridge" connecting the two parts of the building, the vertical movement of the forms are the elements that transform the structure, from static to dynamic, from function to communication.

Residential and Commercial Buildings, Florence, Italy, 2014

These buildings designed for mixed commercial and residential use are part of a recuperative plan for an ex-industrial area in Florence. The two buildings are connected by a sky bridge and a screen in a modern language that uses classical words in a contemporary context. Classical words such as roof and façade, loggia and windows are declined in different ways and forms depending on the uses and needs of the interior spaces and constitute a type of abacus to use in different ways in the two buildings.

The result is a mutation into one large building, complex and articulated, which offers different ways of experiencing the building, utilising dark clay colours and ground floor façade finishes which recall the polished steel trowel plaster of times past combined with new innovative materials such as "technical wood" used for the cladding of the façades which address the main street.

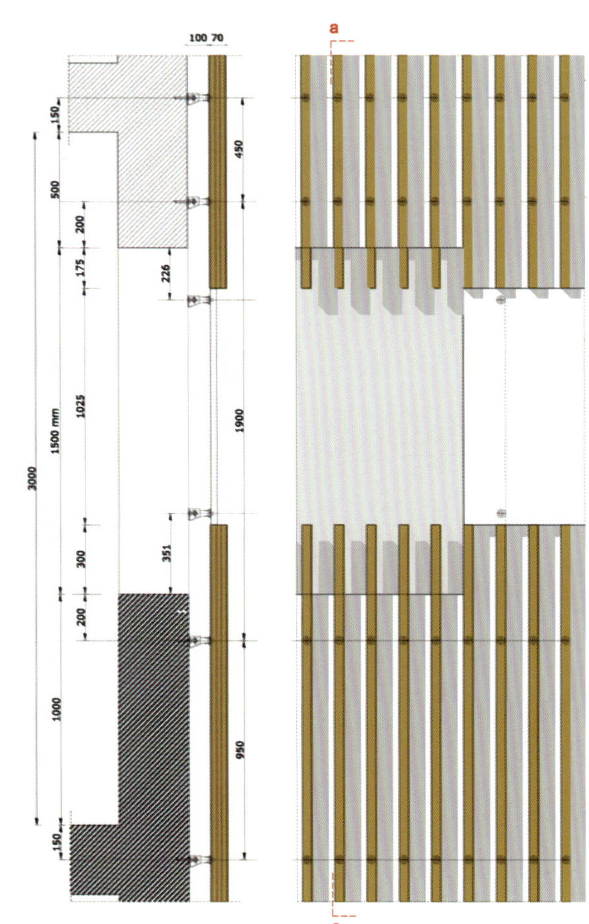

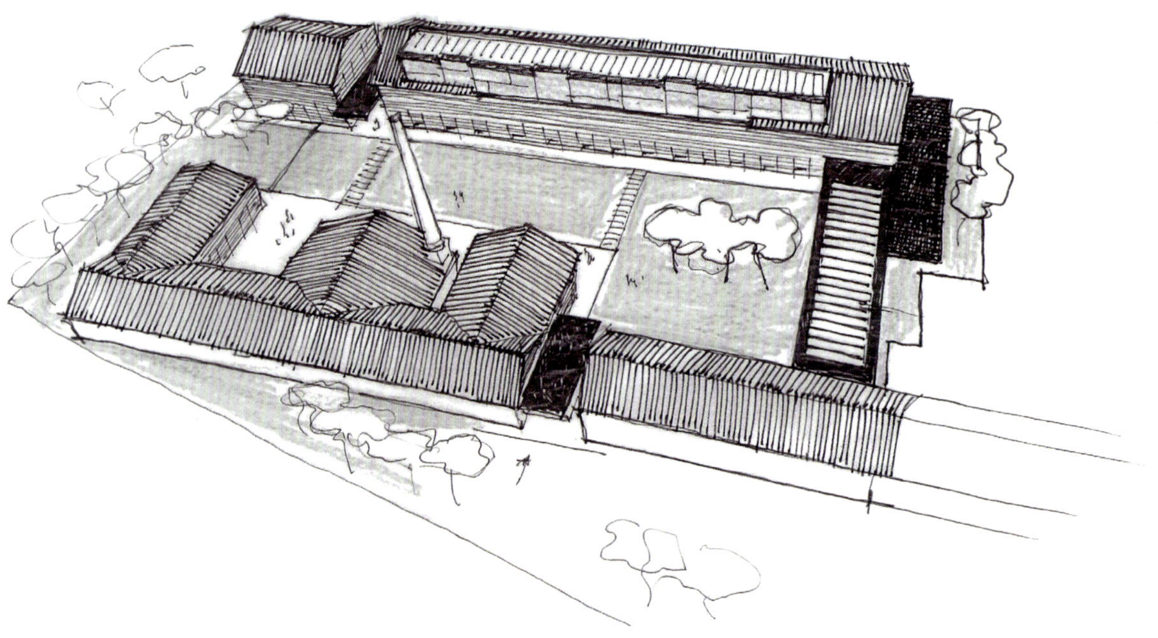

Fabryka, Competition by Invitation, Krakow, Poland, 2014

A project to transformation of an old industrial complex in Krakow, as an example of contemporary architecture that interacts with the context and opportunity to create a new Landmark for the city.

The project involves a mix of functions, connected by arcades and protected passages, and capable of making this area alive and interesting and which allow the maximum exaltation of the architectural quality of existing buildings, above all within. The new volumes are inserted into the existing buildings, linking them together with loggias and glass cases projecting over the industrial buildings and elements of contemporary architecture.

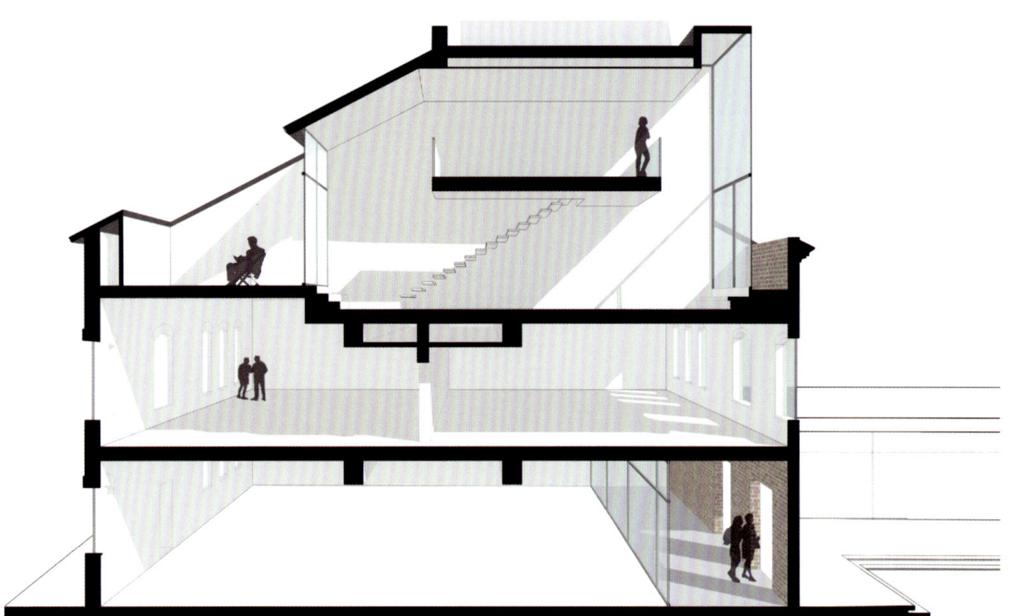

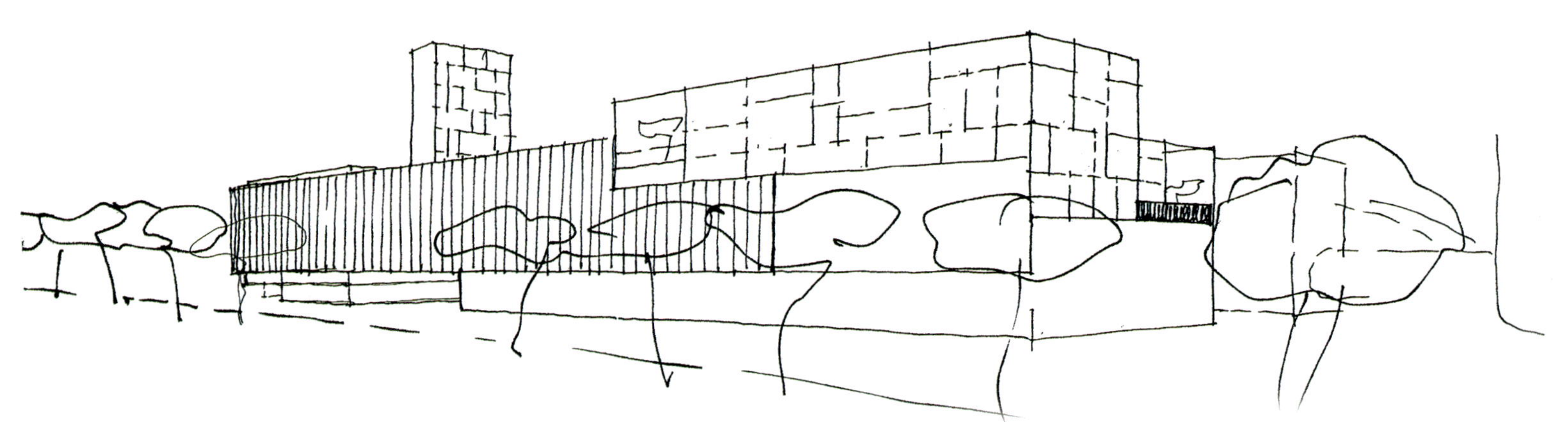

TVP Polish Television Headquarters, Competition, Warsaw, Poland, 2015

National Archives, Competition, Krakow, Poland, 2015

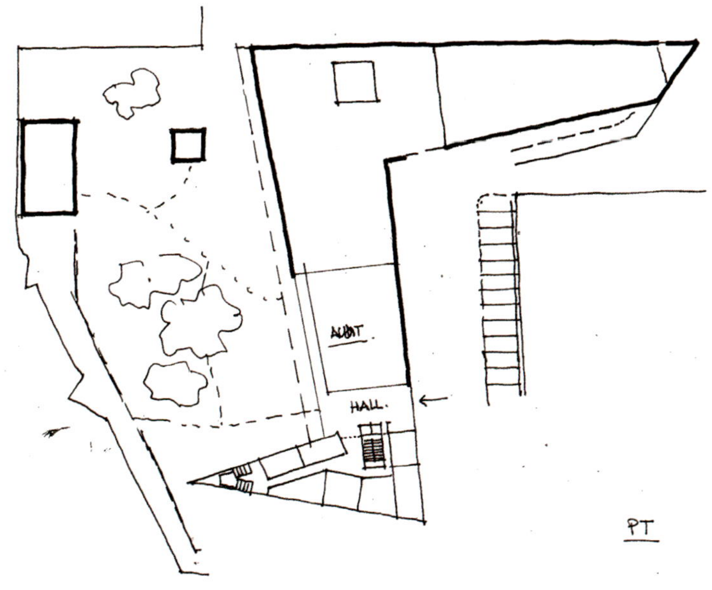
ALBAT.
HALL.
PT

New Town Hall, Competition, First Prize, Krakow, Poland, 2009, Work in Progress

The articulated layout of the construction site, covered with numerous trees which had to be preserved as much as possible, might have seemed a limiting criterion in the design of an important architectural complex, having also too have a high visual impact appropriate to its public role. The building complex designed by Studio Nardi drew its form, its strength and the reason for the dimensions and colour choices to compliment and utilise theses constraints.

A simple, complex, almost natural structure.An architectural organism that functions like a gigantic tree, composed of two independent floors that interact with each other via an articulated system of connections on several levels, through which the vital sap flows along the paths created by its users. Like a natural element, the complex is permeable, a living architecture that fits into its natural setting, so that we imagine the ruddy reflection of the walls on the transparency of the glass, in response to summer brilliance, the contrast with the leafy green branches and the way the buildings merge into the autumn, red as the leaves, and later radiating in rainbow hues from the bright candor of the snow.

Glass is the main material visible on the entire extension of the façades, in a modulation of colourways that indicate

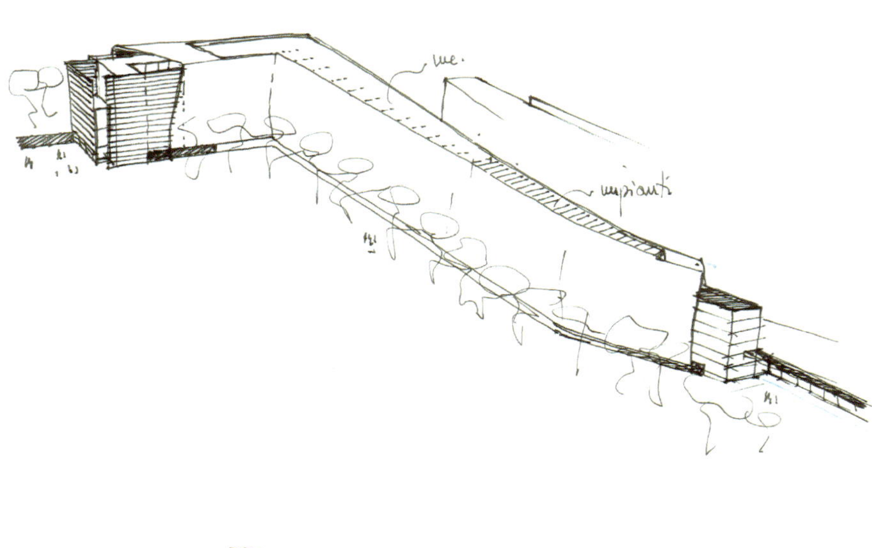

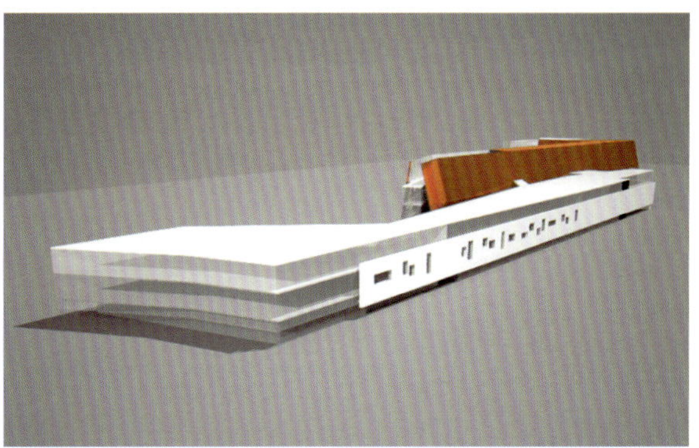

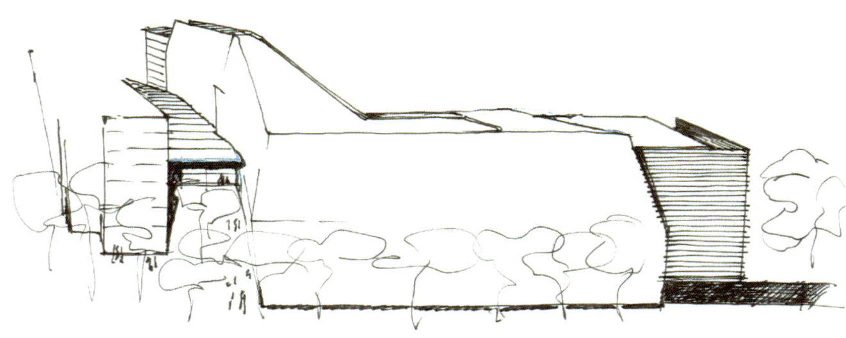

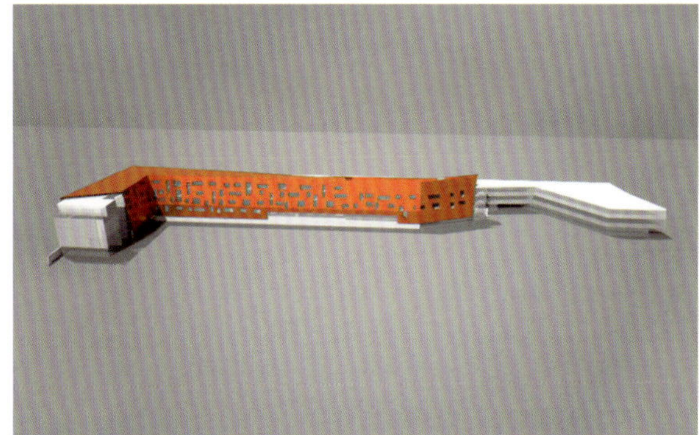

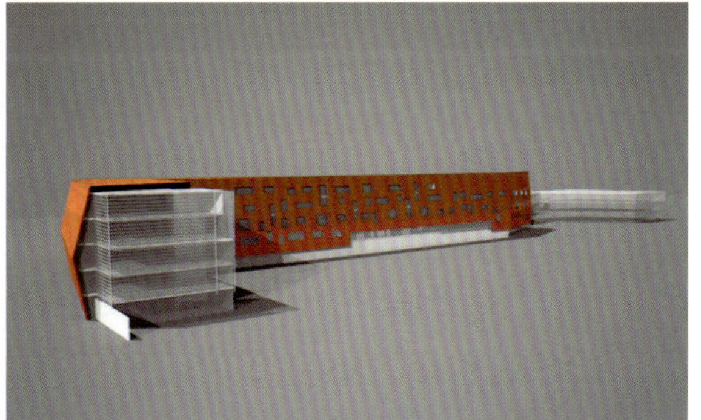

a few key points, like the continuous transparency of the entire ground floor, which makes the two upper floors appear to be floating in the air, or the dark, almost black glass that accentuates the main vertical link, or the light, azure glints that illuminate the offices on the second floor.

Two arcades, set into the façade, each sheltering a small tree, symbolically give the modern, technological, abstract exterior of the building a familiar, domestic character, open and friendly to the citizens.

The other building, located on the south side, which reaches the full 20 metres admissible above ground, stands like a backdrop, set back from the road and creates the immediate perception of the vastness of the complex and its articulation. The sinuous shape of the building is designed around the existing trees that seem to reach inside the common line of connection between the two blocks. The building is panelled on the outside with a ventilated curtain wall in electrically coloured copper iridescent steel panels. This flickering surface is scattered, with irregular geometry, rectangular openings of various sizes that bathe the interiors in light, deep loggias that enclose a little tree or large semitransparent surfaces acting as sun screens to diffuse luminosity.

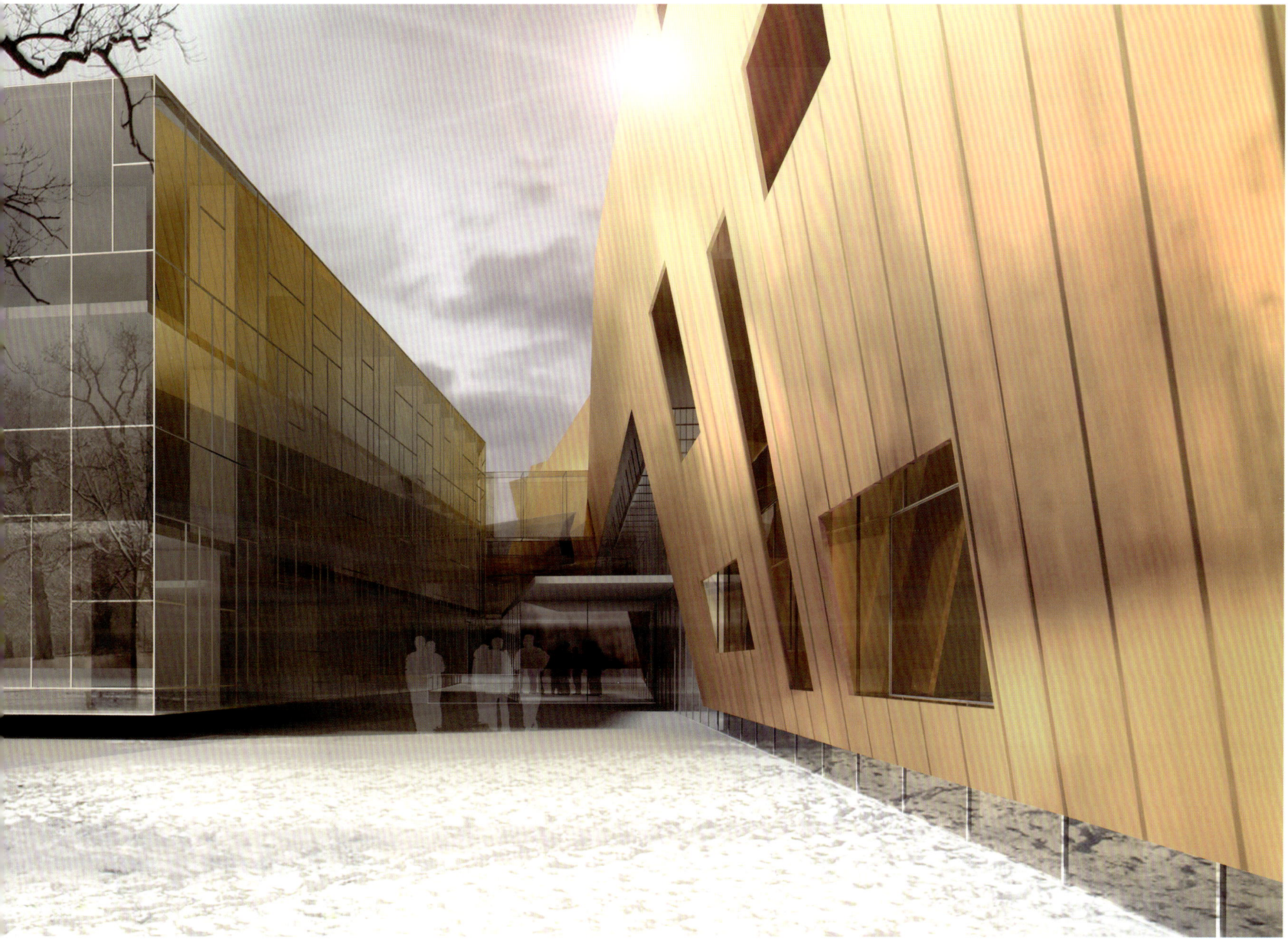

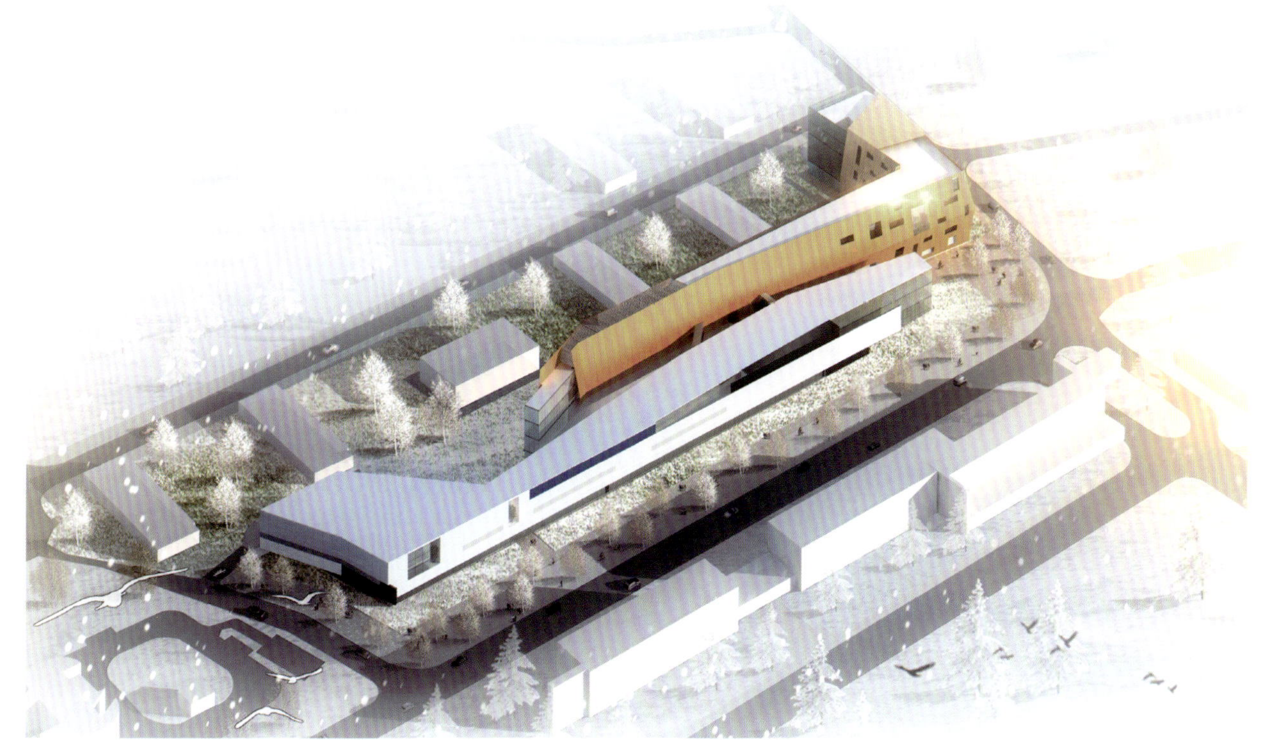

Monticello Resort, Ferragamo Property, Competition by Invitation, San Giustino Valdarno, Italy, 2015

Modern traditionality in the Tuscan countryside.

A village of Neo-Renaissance inspiration, precious and elegant, designed with a combination of traditional and contemporary materials, is arranged around a square split into two levels. Traditional elements translated in a contemporary key, the stone paving, trees (existing), a long wall faced in stone, an atypical fountain that marks the boundary between the two squares at different levels, porticos that accompany and protect the path along the views of commercial activities, the tower, a reference point of communication and the centre of the accommodation complex, the heart of the reception and the system of common spaces.

274

Winery Re Alarico, Carolei, Cosenza, Italy, 2012, Work in Progress

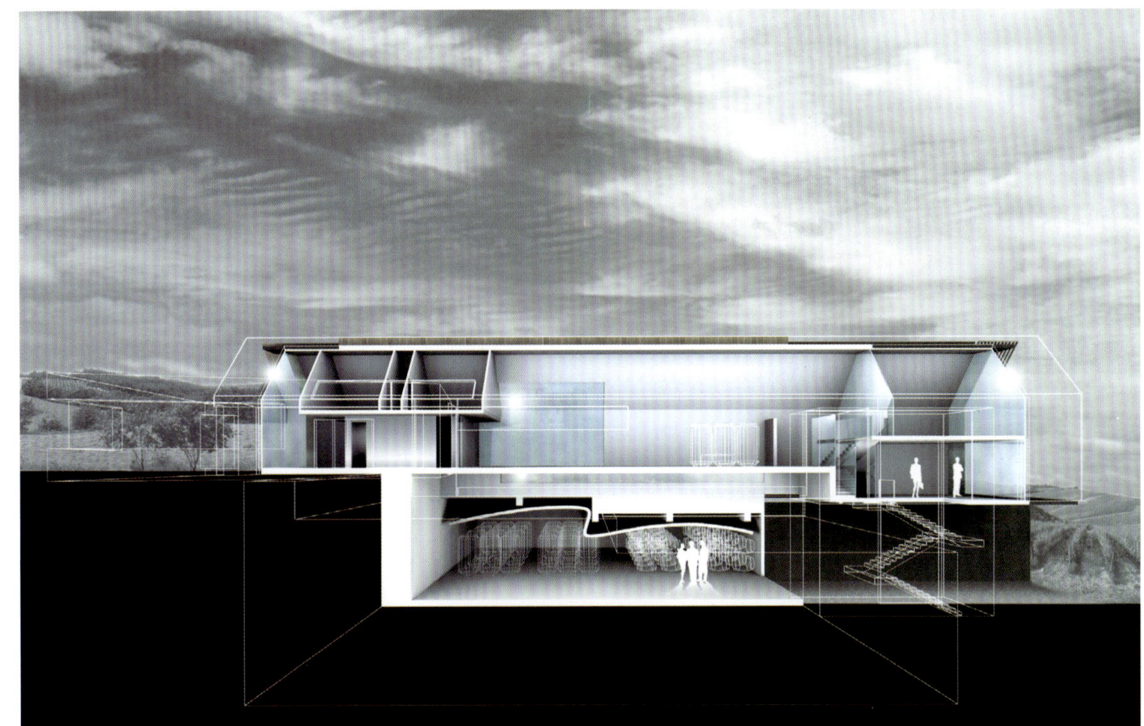

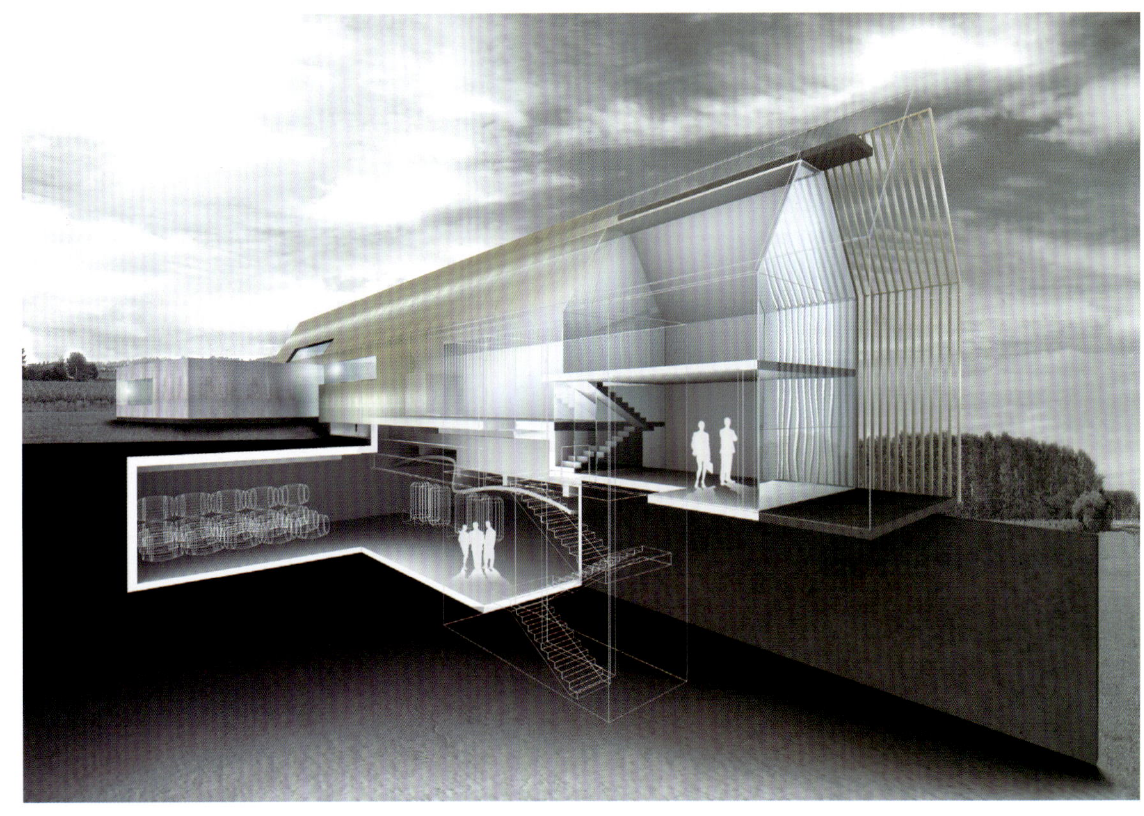

277

Residential Complex, Beijing, China, 2016, Work in Progress

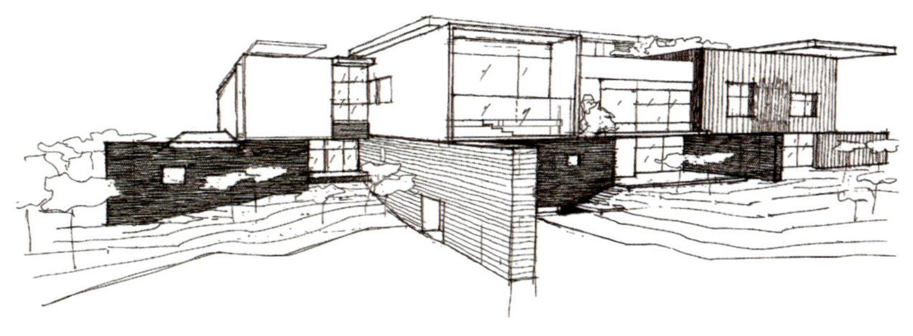

The creation of independent space, a world of floating simultaneous existences. Enjoying nature in a variety of perspectives, the creation of multiple spaces which interact with nature, where the experience of each room with the exterior world is different. This multiplicity is already apparent in the destructualisation of the eight villas; instead of mass there is movement, a series of interconnected volumes, the whole designed to become part of the landscape, independent but not obtrusive. Large and small volumes, screens and voids, all floating upwards from the lake, serene and quiet unique homes designed for the individual in search of tranquility and privacy.

Music Academy, Competition, Admitted to the Second Stage, Krakow, Poland, 2017

Zhejiang Science-Technology University Fashion Institute, Competition, Hangzhou, China, 2017

The buildings stand light, almost suspended on the new landscape, like large trees with open branches linked to each other by pedestrian bridges at various levels.

The new landscape is thought of as a cloak that protects and defines the large surfaces of the ground floor areas destined for multiple activities. The key concept of the University Campus project is to create a park as the foundation for the whole complex; a new natural landscape, designed with the fundamental elements of the area: water (river, ponds, canals), slightly undulating ground levels and native trees. The complex is arranged around large courtyards and large tree-lined squares, which will become the centres for socialisation and open-air activities. All the buildings, thanks to their shape, enjoy multidirectional and very open views, to both the surrounding park environment and into the large green internal areas between one building and the another.

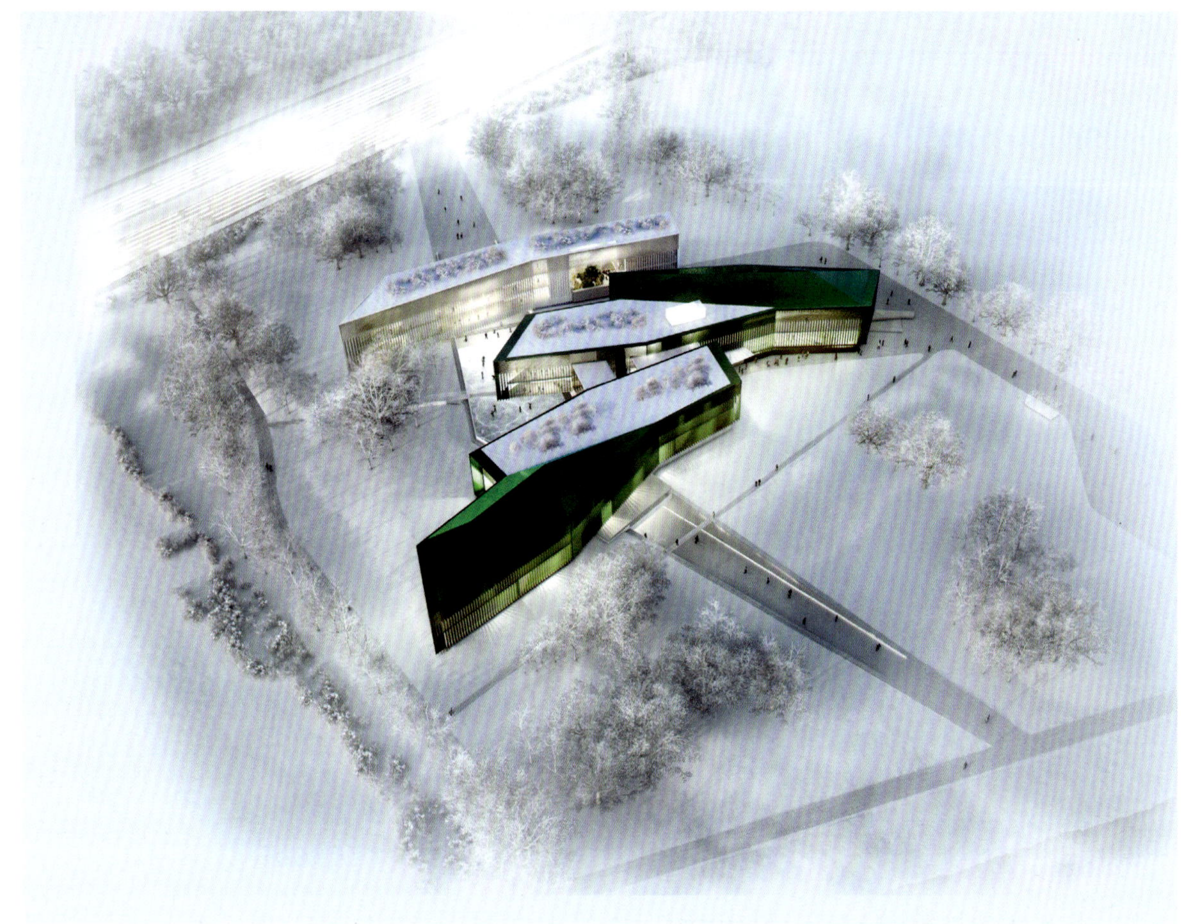

Malopolska Science Centre, Competition, Krakow, Poland, 2017

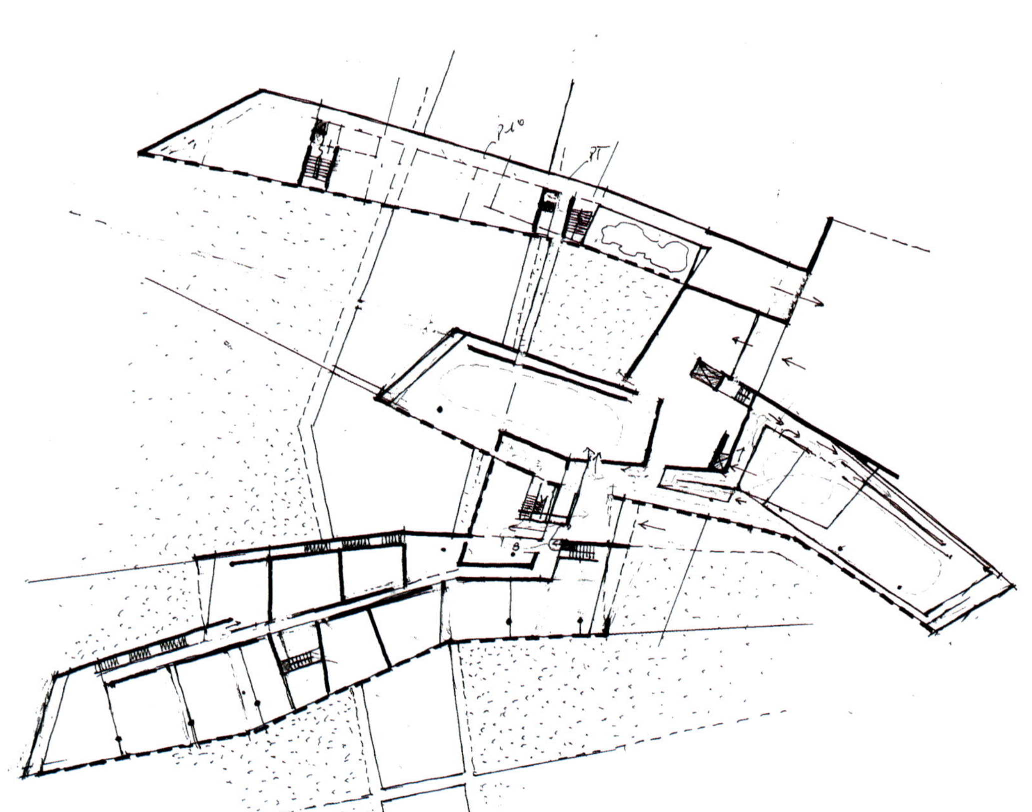

400
350

Fredry Publishing House, Competition, Second Prize, Warsaw, Poland, 2017

The design includes the new functional layout of the entire building and the extension of a part, taking in two different forms and trying to give unity of the complex: one of 19th-century and historical origin, with a Neo-Renaissance symmetrical façade and the other of new conception. The new extension appears as a small jewel set in the existing building.

Its dynamic form seems to give new energy; a new life in the historic building emphasises its value, but the modernisation of the complex does not end in the vibrant form of the new enlargement. The existing interiors, floors, stuccos and newsagents are preserved and integrated with new elements to create new accents and details born from the comparison of the classical matrix with the contemporary one.

A special thank you to Dong Shan Condo, for their contribution to this book.

ACKNOWLEDGEMENTS

Adam Golec

241

Alessandro Ciampi

184–185

Antonio Quattrone

78–79

Carlo Valentini

49, 82–83, 92, 103, 126–137, 144–149,

156–159, 228–231

Claudio Nardi Architects

24–27, 66–69, 84, 102, 104–105,

114–115, 120–125, 164–167, 234–235

Davide Virdis

44–45, 183, 185–186, 202–205

Emre Dorter

60–63

Ezio Manciucca

117

Gabriele Novasi

30–31

Giacomo Salizzoni

78

Jacek Piwowarczyk

241

Jeza Photography

93

Leo Bieber

243

Leonardo Rinaldesi

70–71

Lorenzo Ferroni

138–143

Lorenzo Mennonna

252–255

Lorenzo Vecchia

92, 95

Luca Laurenzi

28–29

Marcin Gierat

90–91, 94, 96–97, 98–101, 243

Mario Ciampi

46–48, 76–77

Massimo Crivellari

86–89

Matteo Piazza

54–55

Michele Biancucci

95

Nicola Cioni

69

Officine Fotografiche

56–59

Pietro Savorelli

38–43, 80–81, 118–119, 256–259

Rafal Sosin

243

Saint Gobain

237–239, 242–243

Santi Caleca

50–53, 117, 119

PHOTO CREDITS